Dramatic Monologue Preaching

DRAMATIC MONOLOGUE PREACHING

ALTON H. McEACHERN

BROADMAN PRESS
Nashville, Tennessee

Unless otherwise noted, Scripture quotations are the author's paraphrase. Scripture quotations marked (KJV) are from the King James Version of the Bible. Scripture quotations marked (RSV) are from the Revised Standard Version of the Bible, copyrighted 1946, 1952, © 1971, 1973.

Some of the sermons in this book have been published before and are used by permission: Hosea, Moses, and Paul, *Drama in Creative Worship*, Everett Robertson, comp. (Nashville: Convention Press, 1978), pp. 10, 12, 14. Howington, McEachern, and Pinson, *Growing Disciples Through Preaching* (Nashville: Broadman Press, 1976), "John, Son of Thunder," pp. 80-88. McEachern, *Here at Thy Table, Lord* (Nashville: Broadman Press, 1977), "Man from Emmaeus," pp. 116-119.

Library of Congress Cataloging in Publication Data

McEachern, Alton H.
  Dramatic monologue preaching.

  1. Baptists—Sermons.   2. Sermons, American.
I. Title.   II. Title: Monologue preaching.
BX6333.M354D7   1984   252'.061   82-82953
ISBN 0-8054-2111-4 (pbk.)

To our children: Suzanne, Michael, Kathryn, Bonnie, and Andrew who have added drama and joy to our lives

Contents

1

Narrative Preaching
Telling the Story

Winston Jones wrote, "Story-telling is the most ancient of the arts, and the most universal."[1]

Preaching is a demanding task. George Buttrick said, "The Lord Christ has his preachers at hard labor." William Barclay insisted that preachers should be chained to their desks four mornings a week and forbidden to rise until they have produced something worthwhile to show for their labors. He also said that if we cannot put fire into our sermons, we should put our sermons in the fire.

No person can approach preaching without some degree of anxiety. D. W. Cleverly Ford has captured this sense of awe in his poem, "The Pulpit."

> Lord, I am afraid of my pulpit.
> I am afraid it is irrelevant.
> I am afraid of the demands it makes
> upon my time and energy.

> And yet it stands there in the church.
> It stands to tell me I must speak.
> It stands to speak as once it spoke to me.
> So I must mount its steps again.

> But what shall I say?
> And how shall I say it?

And who will listen?
And who will benefit? . . .

Lord, I am afraid of my pulpit.
Give me grace to see its relevance.
Give me grace to trust its future.
Give me words to speak thy grace.
Thy grace which called
Thy grace which equipped
Thy grace which I encountered through
the words
Our Saviour uttered: Probing words,
Cleansing words,
Healing words.
The words of the Word made flesh,
spoken from the pulpit of his body.
Jesus Christ, our Lord.[2]

We share a high view of the importance of preaching. Indeed, there is strong biblical argument for the sacramental nature of the preaching event (1 Cor. 1:21-23; Rom. 10:14-15,17). D. M. Baillie contends that "we stand between a memory and a hope, looking backward to the incarnation and forward to the consummation."[3] Inspired preaching makes both events contemporary.

While preaching is demanding, its joys are also great. Carl Sandburg's description of the joy of the street merchant has its parallels in the pastor's joy in preaching:

I know a Jew fish crier down on Maxwell Street
with a voice like a north wind blowing over corn
stubble in January.
He dangles herring before prospective customers

> evincing a joy identical with that of Pavlova dancing.
>
> His face is that of a man terribly glad to be selling fish, terribly glad that God made fish, and customers to whom he may call his wares from a pushcart.[4]

I am "terribly glad" to be a preaching pastor. Buttrick argued that "only the pastor, or a man with pastoral imagination can preach."[5] In his Lyman Beecher Lectures, David H. C. Read contended that "the preacher is a Moses who never gets the children of Israel off his back and doesn't want to. He's not the impresario who says to his secretary, 'Tell that nuisance to go to hell—I'm composing a masterpiece on Christian love.' . . . He is sent from God to live with people, talk with them, listen to them, feel what they feel, and only after he has been through the dusty streets does he mount the pulpit steps. Like his Lord he must be responsive to that tug on the sleeve when he is at his busiest." Read says that the entire Bible stands witness to the pastor-preacher as the "man sent from God."[6]

Dogma Is Drama

Dorothy Sayers made high drama of biblical material. After writing twelve passion plays, she said, "The Christian faith is the most exciting drama that has ever staggered the imagination of man—and the dogma *is* the drama." She found the Gospel narratives anything but dull: "Any journalist hearing it for the first time, would recognize it as news; those who did hear it for the first time did call it . . . good news."[7]

Why then is so much modern preaching anything but interesting and exciting? One reason is that it has lost its dramatic narrative character. The drama we find in the Bible is interesting, universal, and timeless.

One of the great needs of biblical preaching is the need to be contemporary. Narrative preaching is a variant which elaborates the basic biblical materials and creates a sense of contemporaneity. Both the personality and the life situation of the biblical character come alive for the hearer. The dramatic monologue sermon allows the biblical personality to speak in the first person. Listeners may well feel that they are reliving the biblical event. Thus, the Word comes alive in the experience of the hearer to challenge, heal, and redeem. The hearer feels that he is there, a contemporary of the biblical personality and events.

Many times worshipers are not moved by powerful biblical truths because of the truths' familiarity. The listeners have heard the narrative or parable many times since childhood. Some even think of the biblical accounts as fairy tales. This problem calls on the preacher to present his material through new and fresh methods. Narrative preaching is one approach worthy of our consideration.

The theology of the Bible is clothed in the flesh and blood of living characters. Human nature is essentially the same today as it was in biblical times. Some of the characters of the Old and New Testament walk our streets in modern dress, their temperaments and their basic problems the same as our own. Persons like Judas are sticky-fingered treasurers and bankers of our time who enrich themselves at the price of betrayal of trust. Cain still stalks modern parks and alleys. Delilah plies her trade in Paris frock or hot pants. Prejudice did not die with Simon Peter at Caesarea. Salome dances atop French Quarter bars, and Potiphar is preppy. Canaanite fertility cults are practiced by pill-liberated suburban housewives. Modern preaching dare not do less than clothe theological truth in flesh and blood.

Christian worship at its best is dramatic and exciting, though not necessarily theatrical. The church has largely lost its sense of the dramatic nature of the gospel. The ordinances of baptism and Lord's Supper are powerful symbolic presentations of gospel truth. They appeal to all the human senses and have a dramatic quality.

Narrative preaching tends to heighten interest in the message and, thus, enhance communication. While it should not become the only form of preaching, it can add variety and spice to the congregation's sermonic diet.

Narrative preaching is in the finest biblical tradition. Henry Grady Davis contends that the gospel itself is made up principally of narration. It is a series of accounts of people, places, and happenings, not simply rational arguments. Modern preaching appears to have reversed the percentages: while the gospel is nine tenths narration, most of our sermons are nine tenths exhortation.

Most biblical ideas were first presented in story form. It is easier to remember a story than an ordinary sermon or even a poem. The prophets and the author of Genesis 1—11 were master storytellers, as was Jesus. His parables are vivid stories that stick in the mind.

A well-told story still has great appeal. Children beg their parents to read or tell them a story. Adults almost universally enjoy "a good story." Theater and the television industry are built on human interest in stories. A good story can capture the essence of an event and hold it before the hearers for either entertainment or instruction.

The preacher will be wise to capitalize on the dramatic nature of the gospel and our natural interest in drama. Jesus made people see the truth by simple stories. The modern preacher's task is much the same. Skillfully done, narrative preaching, including the dramatic monologue, can improve the effective communication of the gospel. It gets and holds the congregation's attention. It creates a high level of interest in the message. Narrative preaching can be an effective teaching device, conveying Bible knowledge, as well as stirring the emotions and moving the will of the hearers.

Considerations in Narrative Preaching

The use of imagination has an important place in narrative preaching. This type of sermon calls for filling in the gaps not covered in the biblical narrative. The preacher has more opportunity to make use of his imagination in dramatic preaching than in other types. He is at liberty to create the feelings and emotions of the character, as well as to describe the setting. He will be careful that his imagination does not violate the biblical account.

The narrative sermon can create suspense. People will listen eagerly. Spurgeon called the use of imagination in preaching "surprise power."

I have found that the fruit of critical Bible study can often be introduced into a sermon by imagining the life situation of a biblical character.

One problem in narrative preaching is the danger of anachronism. By this, I mean putting things into the character's life and speech that could not have been true to his time. It is very easy to let untimely references or jargon slip into the narration. This is always a literary problem. The King James Version of the Bible speaks of candlesticks instead of lampstands. Shakespeare had a clock strike in his play *Julius Caesar*, though clocks had not yet been invented. One must be sure to check the historical accuracy of the facts included in narrative preaching.

This type preaching also requires careful research and preparation on the part of the preacher. You will want to be as familiar as possible with the times in which the character lived, striving for historical accuracy. The objective of confronting persons with the claims of the gospel requires the preacher's very best effort in both preparation and delivery.

How-to

You will want to make careful research notes, giving attention to your sources. After the basic research is complete, give it some time to mellow. The entire sermon idea may be put on a back burner until a central theme surfaces. Frederick Speakman says that it often requires a month for him to write a dramatic monologue sermon.

Once you've found the key for the sermon, organize your facts and narrative around it. Do not be afraid to eliminate good material in favor of the best. Ideally, a sermon should run not more than twenty to twenty-five minutes. You can't have a character relate all the facts you know about him in that brief span. Therefore, you will choose only the most important facts which fit your theme. Severe pruning can make the sermon more effective. No one will be impressed by being told all the preacher knows at a single sitting. Remember to deal with only the central aspect of the character.

You may choose to write out your manuscript or use what Clyde Fant calls the "oral manuscript" in preparation for delivery. Writing will help to polish phrases and maintain a conversational style. Use short sentences and simple strong words. Write the introduction and conclusion carefully and commit them to memory.

The introduction sets the scene and introduces the speaking character, as well as those to whom he is speaking. This helps prepare the congregation for what is to follow.

Write out the narrative in simple language. You will want to use active colorful verbs and vivid descriptions of people and places. Always be faithful to the biblical material.

I find that the sermon needs to be rehearsed both mentally and verbally in order to have it clearly in mind. There is hardly any way to speak effectively in the first person or to deliver an exciting narrative while reading from extensive notes or a manuscript. It is not necessary to memorize the sermon word for word, though a few persons have such a gift. Only the key passages need to be memorized—the pegs on which the narrative hangs. A key word or phrase can act as a transitional device and trigger the preacher's memory to recall the next section of the sermon. W. E. Sangster contended that the preacher should learn to "think paragraphically."

In delivery the narrative sermon may be addressed to an imaginary person. Dramatic techniques of flashback and reverie may be employed as well. Conversational tone is usually best for use in this type preaching. However, conversational speech need not lack excitement and emotion.

You may want to create the scene verbally or on occasion make proper use of lighting, costume, and makeup. It appears that the use of costume is more effective in the evening service than in the morning. Children, youth, and young adults have a greater appreciation for the use of costume than do middle or older adults.

One of the weaknesses in dramatic preaching is at the point of the application of biblical truth. The application has to be self-evident or implicit rather than explicit. It is awkward for the preacher to step out of character and apply the sermon's spiritual truths to modern-life situations. Most hearers are more capable of making their own application than we preachers think.

One way to begin narrative preaching is not to attempt an entire sermon. Start with a vivid introduction to a more conventional sermon. You may try painting a word picture of a biblical scene, such as Peter's call beside the Sea of Galilee or the siege of Jerusalem or the wailing of the songless Israelite captives in Babylon. After you feel comfortable with the method, it can be expanded and used for a full-length sermon.

The Advent and Easter seasons lend themselves naturally to dramatic preaching. It can be great fun and may provide a fresh and effective tool for communicating the gospel.

The late J. Wallace Hamilton of Florida gave us some words which can be aptly applied to narrative preaching. He wrote: "Clarity, poetry, vitality! We must make it clear; we must make it sing; and above it all we must make it live."[8]

Notes

1. Winston Jones, *Preaching and the Dramatic Arts* (New York: The Macmillan Co., 1948), p. 106.

2. D. W. Cleverly Ford, *Preaching Today* (London: Epworth Press, 1969), prologue. Used by permission.

3. D. M. Baillie, *Theology of the Sacraments* (New York: Charles Scribner's Sons, 1957), p. 102.

4. From CHICAGO POEMS by Carl Sandburg, copyright 1916 by Holt, Rinehart and Winston, Inc.; renewed 1944 by Carl Sandburg. Reprinted by

permission of Harcourt Brace Jovanovich, Inc.

    5. George Buttrick, *Sermons Preached in a University Church* (Nashville: Abingdon, 1959), p. 7.

    6. David H. Read, *Sent from God* (Nashville: Abingdon, 1974), pp. 69-70.

    7. Dorothy Sayers, *The Greatest Drama Ever Staged* (London: Hodder and Stoughton, 1938), pp. 17, 24.

    8. J. Wallace Hamilton, *Still the Trumpet Sounds* (Old Tappan: Fleming H. Revell, 1970), p. 159.

2
Herald of the King—John the Baptist
Luke 1:5-24,57-66,76-80

Come, let us journey to Jericho, the oldest town on earth which dates back to 7800 BC, almost ten thousand years ago. It was the city conquered by Joshua. In New Testament times, it was the city of blind Bartimaeus and a sycamore tree-climbing Zacchaeus. Jericho is located five miles north of the Dead Sea. It is built at the site of Elisha's fountain or spring which continues to flow copiously until this day.

The year is AD 39. In our imagination we've come for a visit with Joel, a blacksmith of Jericho. His shop is located on the north side of town, near the spring and the mound which covers the ruins of the ancient city. The entrance to Joel's shop gapes open like the mouth of a panting dog. His bellows wheeze asthmatically. Joel stands in the heat, stripped to his waist. He is short, stocky, and stooped. His bald head is wet with perspiration, and the ring of white hair about his temples looks like a semi-halo. His huge hands are gnarled and calloused. They hold the tongs and hammer at the anvil. He doesn't appear to ever make an idle blow. Every strike counts, and the anvil rings out melodically. Boys play in the narrow street in front of the shop, always fascinated with the blacksmith's art.

As we stand in the doorway, Joel spies us. He stills the ringing hammer almost automatically and drops the piece of hot iron to sizzle into a crock of black water. Mopping his brow with his forearm, he approaches with a broad smile which reveals the loss of a front tooth.

"Welcome, friends, to Jericho and Joel's lowly shop. Peace be with you."

We reply, "Shalom."

"Come out here, let's sit out beneath the sycamore." He wipes his face, this time with the underside of his long apron and sits down on a palm log in the shade of the tree.

"So you want to know about John the baptizer, do you? I'll be glad to tell you all I know, and that's quite a bit. I was one of his disciples. But first, let's have a cold drink. Miriam, bring fresh water for my friends.

"John began his ministry in these parts when Pontius Pilate was governor of Judea, the time that the word of the Lord came to John bar-Zechariah. He was an authentic prophet. He did his baptizing just to the east of here where there's a ford across the Jordan River.

"To go a bit further back, let me tell you about Zechariah, John's father. He was a priest who served his turn in the Temple in Jerusalem. Once, while he was on duty and burning incense before the altar, he saw the angel Gabriel. The angel said to Zechariah, 'Your prayers have been answered. Your wife, Elizabeth, shall have a son. You shall call his name John, for he shall be the gift of God.' Zechariah was frightened and protested to the angel that he and his wife were old people, well beyond the age of having children. They had prayed long that God would bless their home.

"The angel said, 'Because you have not believed what I have told you, I'll give you a sign, and that is you'll not be able to speak until the child is born.'

"In due course, sure enough, Elizabeth did conceive and bore a son. When the child was born, the neighbors and kinsmen rejoiced at such a miracle. They said, 'Let's name him Zechariah after his father.' Elizabeth protested, 'No. We are going to call him John.'

"'Let's ask his father,' said Elizabeth. They gave Zechariah a writing tablet, and he wrote on it, 'His name is John.' And all of a sudden, Zechariah's voice returned. He was no longer dumb, but began to speak and to praise God saying, 'This child shall be called the prophet of the Most High. He will go before the Lord to prepare his way!'

"You see, I was related to John as was Jesus on his mother's side. We were all cousins, though I never figured out whether it was first, second, or third. John spent his early years with his parents in a little village called Ain Karim, to the west of the city of Jerusalem. By the time John was about ten, Zechariah and Elizabeth had both died. He had no brothers, and there were no other close family members. My father would have taken John in, but there were eleven of us children already, and it was hard enough to make ends meet. My father took John to a settlement south of here, at Qumran. The community was run by a Jewish sect who called themselves the Essenes. They do not believe in marriage, so they propagate their beliefs by adopting male children and rearing them in the faith. John spent the rest of his childhood in this desert area.

"Now, the Essenes are very fine men. They are quite strict in their discipline. I'm sure this was reflected in John's manner of life and preaching. The Essenes lead a simple life. They do not trade or make weapons. They own no slaves and refuse to take oaths. They wear white clothing and lead a common life of mutual support. They do have a passion for cleanliness which is second only to their love of the law and Scriptures. They certainly have the finest library in this part of the world. The Essenes look forward with keen anticipation to the coming of Messiah. Their motto is from the scroll of Isaiah, 'Prepare in the wilderness a way. Make straight in the desert a highway for God.'

"Obviously, my cousin John was influenced by the Essenes, their devotion to the Scripture and their demand for ethical living. Yet, in his own beliefs, John went far beyond them. You must understand that there had been no prophet in Israel for hundreds of years, and suddenly, the word of the Lord came to John. He leaped on the stage of Hebrew history, full grown and fully armed! You should have heard him preach. He was about thirty-one years old.

He dressed like a common son of the desert, wearing a great camel's hair robe which kept him warm against the night's chill. He ate the ordinary fare of the desert folk, fried locusts and wild honey.

John's voice was harsh and strong, like thunder and with a ring like my anvil. It was well suited to preaching in the open air. He preached rapidly and emphatically. His manner was both abrupt and authoritative. In moments of ecstasy, he soared like an eagle and in moments of humility he was like a tamed eagle—but always an eagle. John didn't have much of a sense of humor, and he wasn't noted for his patience. He was rather impatient with evil. He certainly stuck to his theme, 'The kingdom of God.'

"It was astonishing, you know, his baptizing Jews. That was simply unheard of. Oh, it's true that when a proselyte comes into the Jewish faith, he is circumcised and baptized and then goes to the Temple to offer sacrifice. But the idea of baptizing good Jews, children of Abraham, was absolutely unheard of.

"The fame of John's preaching spread like a desert wildfire. I closed my shop and went out to hear him. To be perfectly candid, I was curious about this distant kinsman of mine who was such a sudden sensation as a preacher. Oh, the crowds came. They came from Jericho, Jerusalem, and all Judea. All kinds of people put in an appearance. There were despised tax collectors and soldiers. There were the arrogant Pharisees and Sadducees. John's message attracted the rich and the poor, the high and the low. Even priests came to hear him.

"John's preaching was first of all a summons to

repent. Looking at the haughty Pharisees, he said, 'You brood of vipers! Who warned you to flee from the wrath to come?' His preaching fell like hammer blows on consciences and made them receptive to the working of God's Spirit. He preached that we should be baptized as an act of repentance and preparation for the coming of the kingdom of God. He was insistent that the kingdom was at hand. We Hebrews are so proud of being God's chosen people. John punctured our pride when he said, 'God is able from these stones to raise up children to Abraham!'

"John's preaching had about it an ethical demand as well. He said, 'Bear fruits that befit repentance.' His hearers would come asking, 'What should we do?' He said, 'If you have two coats, share one; if you have plenty of food, share with those who have none.' Tax collectors asked, 'What shall we do?' John replied, 'Collect no more than is appointed.' Soldiers asked, 'What shall we do?' John answered, 'Rob no one by violence or false accusation and be content with your wages.'

"John's preaching also contained the fiery threat of judgment. His figures of speech were vivid indeed. He said, 'The axe is laid at the root of barren trees. They will be cut down and burned in the fire.' He said, 'The fan of the threshing floor is separating the chaff from the wheat. The chaff will be burned in a consuming fire.' It was hard to miss his meaning or be very comfortable with it. He preached like the prophet Elijah. Indeed, some thought he was Elijah, returned to life to precede the Messiah. John said, 'No, I am only a voice, crying in the wilderness. Get ready, the King is coming. His kingdom is at hand.' Some thought that John might be the Messiah. But, he said, 'I am not worthy to untie the sandals of the one who is coming after me.' Well, his preaching certainly excited our expectation and resulted in many confessing their sins. John baptized hundreds in the Jordan River.

"Now, don't get me wrong, while there was the unmistakable fiery note of judgment in his preaching, John was no prophet of doom. He preached the good news of the kingdom of God. His preaching was shot through with promise.

"One day we were listening to John preach and watching as he baptized new converts in the river. The last one coming to be baptized that day was Jesus bar-Joseph from Nazareth in Galilee. When John saw him, he said, 'Behold, the Lamb of God who takes away the sin of the world. This is he of whom I spoke, the one who is greater than I, who shall come after me.' John did not feel worthy to baptize his cousin, Jesus, but Jesus insisted. You know, Jesus' baptism was quite an endorsement of John's ministry as the authentic forerunner of the Messiah. It was also a point of identification with humanity, our sin, sorrow, and suffering. Surely, for Jesus himself, it must have been the high point in his own realization that he was the Messiah.

"I will never forget what it was like that day. About the time Jesus was baptized and came up out of the water, there were sudden clouds and a clap of thunder. A streak of summer lightning flashed across the sky. There seemed to be a voice in the rumblings.

John later told me that he heard the voice say, 'This is my beloved Son in whom I am well pleased.' Believe me, it was an unforgettable moment. It was as though the shoulders of God were stooping under the weight of our sin.

"Would you believe that John's ministry only lasted about six months? One day the soldiers came, not to hear him preach, but to arrest him and to take him to Herod's winter palace. John had condemned that fox of a ruler for marrying his brother Philip's wife, Herodias. She was also the daughter of Herod's half brother. John said right out, 'It is not lawful for you to have her.' It's not safe to talk to despots like that! John was thrown into the dungeon of the Fortress Machaerus. I was among John's disciples who were permitted to visit him on occasion. We found him in deep reflection and somewhat puzzled by all that had happened. He sent us to Jesus with a question, 'Are you the one who is coming or shall we look for another?' Jesus sent us back to John with a message, 'Go and tell John what you have heard and seen. The blind receive their sight, the deaf hear, the lame walk, lepers are cleansed, the dead are raised, and the poor have the good news preached to them.' This was all the encouragement John needed. John said, 'He must increase, I must decrease.' The green-eyed monster of envy never found a place to grow in the heart of John the Baptist.

"Jesus paid a tremendously high tribute to John. He asked the people, 'What went you out to see in the wilderness, a reed shaken by the wind, a man in city clothes or a prophet? Yes, you heard a prophet. He is the Elijah who was to precede the Messiah.'

"Not long after that, King Herod threw a birthday party and invited all the important people in the kingdom to his winter palace at Machaerus. There were the usual goings on, including toasts to the Emperor, to Herod, and to all the celebrities present. Salome, the daughter of Philip and Herodias, danced before the group. This vulgar dance inflamed the guests and earned their hearty applause. Herod, apparently feeling his wine, swore an oath that he would grant her anything she wanted. Salome went out and asked her mother what she should request. When she returned, the young girl asked for the head of John the Baptist on a platter! King Herod must have been stunned, but he had to keep his stupid oath, and so the request was granted. After it was all over, we were given permission to bury John's body. It was the darkest day in my life.

"When Jesus received word of John's execution, he took up John's ministry and even preached his text, 'Repent, for the kingdom is at hand.'

"Jesus paid John the Baptist the highest compliment. He called him the greatest man born of a woman, and then he said that the least person in the kingdom of heaven is greater than John."

3
Simon the Grateful Leper
Luke 19:35-44

This Palm Sunday lend me your imagination. Let us hear an eyewitness account of the triumphal entry.

"Greetings! I am Simon of Bethany. My neighbors call me Simon, the grateful leper. You know my story, I'm sure. Jesus healed ten of us of that dread disease. As a result, I became a follower of the rabbi from Galilee. I believe he is the Messiah of God.

"You also know about some of my neighbors in the village of Bethany: Lazarus, whom Jesus raised from the dead; and Lazarus's sisters, Martha and Mary.

"You see, Jesus spent the past six days as their guest in Bethany. Last night after sundown (and the end of sabbath), I had Jesus as the guest of honor at a banquet at my house. The village notables were present, including Lazarus. Due to his being raised by Jesus, Lazarus has become our most celebrated citizen. I also invited some longtime friends to the banquet. Jesus has made such a difference in my life—both by his healing and by his gospel. I wanted my neighbors to meet the Master. I knew that once they felt the warmth of his personality and heard his gospel of the kingdom, they might become believers as well. Not that I was trying to manipulate my friends; I was simply anxious for them to have the opportunity to know Jesus.

"At the banquet Martha served, of course. As I indicated, Lazarus was our second guest of honor. I expected Mary to help Martha, but she was not present. Mary could never be counted on when it came to domestic work. Oh, she did it, but never happily. No matter! The banquet was going well. The roast lamb was superb, cooked to a turn. Everyone seemed to be enjoying themselves. Though the group was diverse, it was relaxed. I could hardly wait for Jesus to give his after-dinner address and then answer questions from the group as rabbis do.

"We were all enjoying our dinner when I noticed Mary come into the room. She had something in her hands. *Well,* thought I, *she has decided to help serve after all. Well and good.*

"Mary walked behind my couch and out of my line of vision.

"Suddenly, the room was filled with a magnificent fragrance. It was apparent above all the aromas of oriental spices and cooking. The fragrance fairly assaulted our senses!

"Every eye turned toward Mary. She was standing at Jesus' feet, anointing them with this costly perfume from a broken alabaster vial.

"Then, there was an audible gasp from the men at the table. Mary reached up and pulled the bronze pin from her hair. Her jet black tresses came cascading down below her waist. Mingling her salty tears with the sweet perfume, she bathed Jesus' feet and wiped them with her hair.

"It was simply shocking! No decent woman would loose her hair in the presence of any man except her husband, and then only in the privacy of their home.

"What could all this mean? I mused as we sat in stunned silence. Then it dawned on me. This was no indecent display of affection. It was love's extravagance expressing itself in beautiful gratitude. Mary stood totally unself-conscious. She saw only her Master and must have felt only deep thanks for what Jesus had done for her and for her family!

"In the next moment, I found myself looking inward. Jesus means a great deal to me. I owe my health and my faith to him. I have been grateful—even my neighbors are aware of that. Yet, I've never found any appropriate, much less extravagant, way of expressing my gratitude to Jesus. Tell me, have you ever given him anything sacrificially? Have you ever given your gratitude such vivid and extravagant expression as Mary did?

"Toward the close of that long minute of stunned silence, I became aware that some of Jesus' disciples were reacting differently from me. You could tell by the expression on some faces they were indignant. Simon Peter was usually the group's spokesman. However, last night it was Judas Iscariot who spoke up. 'What a foolish waste of good money!' said he. 'That perfume could have been sold for a small fortune . . . and given to the poor.' Judas' last phrase had the bearing of an afterthought and the ring of false piety, I thought. Strange, how differently we react to the same event, isn't it?

"It was obvious from the look on Jesus' face that he was fully aware of what some of his disciples were thinking, even before Judas spoke.

"'Look at her!' said Jesus. (No one could look at anyone else. Every eye was riveted on her.) 'Don't criticize her. She has done a good thing. You will not always have me with you. Mary has anointed me for my burial.'

"For his burial? What could he mean by that? Well, last night was a night to remember. I'm very sure that every guest there will long recall that experience!

"But let me tell you about what happened this morning. Shortly after daybreak we were up. I went over to Lazarus's house to ask how much longer the Master would be in Bethany.

"Some of Jesus' disciples were asking him where they would eat the Passover feast. Jesus told three of them to go into the city (Jerusalem) to such and such a house and tell the owner their Master would eat the Passover there. He asked them to arrange for the large upper room and buy the necessary provisions for the festival.

"Jesus delegated three other disciples to go into the neighboring village of Bethphage to the house of a certain man who had a young colt. Jesus said they should tell the owner their rabbi needed the animal and would return it soon.

"The disciples did as Jesus instructed them and

soon returned with the animal. They placed their cloaks on the colt, and Jesus mounted it. He rode out of Bethany toward Jerusalem.

"The word of Lazarus's raising had stirred all sorts of interest and curiosity among the people. Many were now convinced that this miracle proved Jesus to be Messiah. So widespread was this feeling that the high priest in Jerusalem determined not only to kill Jesus but to return Lazarus (the evidence) to his grave as well.

"The excited crowd thronged after Jesus and ahead of him. As far as the eye could see, they crowded the narrow road around the Mount of Olives. The disciples with Jesus were obviously concerned about his security. It was a perfect set-up for an assassin. He could do his dirty work and then melt into the crowd again. Stocky Simon Peter served as Jesus' bodyguard. He led the colt, constantly scanning the sea of faces for any troublemaker. Peter kept his right hand beneath his tunic, gripping the hilt of a short sword.

"However, Jesus had nothing to fear from that crowd this morning. They were shouting hosannahs: 'Hail to the King! Blessed is he who comes in the name of the Lord.' They chanted these cheers over and over. The mood of the crowd was exhilarating. It was reflected on Jesus' face as well. The crowd's excitement was part festive spirit and part religious fervor.

"Suddenly, I recalled a portion of Scripture I'd memorized long ago in synagogue school: 'Fear not, daughter of Zion; behold your king is coming, sitting on a ass' colt!' That's what it all meant. This was a sign that Jesus is the Messiah!

"As we rounded the Mount of Olives, Jerusalem stretched before us—golden Jerusalem, the walled city of God, with the towers of Fortress Antonio and the Temple complex on Mount Moriah. The Temple's polished bronze doors glistened in the morning sunlight.

"Jesus' mood suddenly melted into tears! It is a strange sight to see a grown man cry. He lifted his voice in lament and predicted the city's destruction—not peace.

"There was the sound of thunder in a clear sky. Some standing near Jesus said it was a deep-throated rumble like a voice. The voice said, 'I have glorified thy name.' What could it all mean?

"Roman soldiers guarded the entrance to the city. They let Jesus and his party in, then drew their broadswords to make a fence of steel. They turned the throng back from the Golden Gate—to prevent a riot, they said . . . or a coronation!

"As I walked away I caught a whiff of the perfume from last night. 'Anointed me for my burial,' Jesus had said. What could that mean? What does this day hold—and this week? What will come of it all, I wonder? Somehow the atmosphere seems strangely oppressive. 'Anointed . . . for burial?'"

4
Despised Matthew
Matthew 9:9-13

"Simon, old friend, how grand it is to see you! I never expected to be home in Capernaum again. The gospel has carried me far, and everywhere I go I find those who are believers in the risen Christ. I've been in Antioch in Syria, across Asia Minor, into Greece, over into North Africa, and Ethiopia, and finally to Rome. Every place I go I find some who make the sign of the fish, some who believe in Jesus our Lord. Even in Caesar's household there are those who hold to the faith. It is most encouraging, indeed. In fact, it is almost unbelievable how rapidly the gospel news has spread in our lifetime.

"My, but Capernaum hasn't changed much. It still has its quiet charm and unforgettable setting, with the Sea of Galilee to the south of it and the cliffs of Syria on the east. Tiberias, the Roman city to the west looks much the same, as well.

"The new synagogue here in Capernaum is simply dazzling. Is it true it was built by the centurion whose boy Jesus healed? What a wonderful expression of a father's gratitude to God. I shall never forget that man's faith. It is a lovely memorial. May it stand for centuries.

"Simon, I must confess that a thousand fond memories flood my mind as I walk these familiar shores. It seemed as though in my mind I could still see Jesus sitting on the hillside delivering his sermon or feeding the five thousand or preaching from a boat just off from shore.

"The old tax house here in Capernaum looks much as I remembered it. I well remember when I sat as tax collector there. *Publicans* they called us. It's a fallen word you know. In the Roman language, Latin, it's a perfectly good word. It means a public servant or one who handles public funds. But among our Jewish neighbors, it became the most despised word in the language, second only to *Samaritan*.

"When I was young, I got into trouble with the law and made a bad record with the Romans. One day I was brought in, pardoned of my crimes and misdemeanors and made a publican. Well, I became well-to-do as the Jewish collector of Roman taxes, but I paid a heavy price for my prosperity. Gold is a poor substitute for friends. I had very few, really only you and Zacchaeus in Jericho. Tell me, how is he? I understand he waters that sycamore tree where he met the Master. It's a shame he can't water himself, short fellow!

"I remember hearing Jesus many times from a distance. I longed to know him and sense the forgiveness that he talked about. Imagine my surprise when one day he stopped at my customhouse and called me to follow him. I gladly gave up everything in order to be his disciple.

"My fellow tax officials were exasperated at my

decision. For, you see, I had been right efficient in my job. The Romans, as you recall, farmed their taxes out, and we were allowed to keep whatever we could collect above the levied assessment. Taxes were multiplied to be sure. There was a ground tax which was 10 percent of the crops and 20 percent of all the wine, oil, and fruit a man produced. There was an income tax and a sales tax; a poll tax and customs on imports and exports. I was also responsible for all kinds of tolls on bridges, the use of the harbor, roads, rivers, and dams. We would tax a man's cart and the beast that pulled it, its wheels and its axle. The beauty of it was that we had the right of search and that we were backed up by Roman law and Roman soldiers.

"Actually, it's little wonder that the tax collectors were classified by the common people, along with murderers and robbers, as criminals.

"Simon, do you remember the feast I gave? Only our friends were there, fellow outcasts, though a prominent and financially successful lot. The Pharisees criticized Jesus for daring to enter my house and eat with the likes of us. I shall never forget his reply. He said, 'The well have no need of a physician.'

"These have been busy days, my brother. I've begun to write the logia. These are the teachings of Jesus which I've managed to set down in writing. I hope that my writing down the sayings of Jesus will give them a wide reading. Perhaps in time someone will add to these teachings and sayings the story of Jesus' life and death and resurrection. My purpose in writing, however, has been basically to convince my fellow Jews that Jesus is the Messiah. Yes, I'll be glad to read a portion of what I've written. Here let me move over beside the lamp where the light is better.

"And seeing the multitudes, he went up into a mountain: and when he was set, his disciples came unto him: And he opened his mouth, and taught them, saying, Blessed are the poor in spirit: for theirs is the kingdom of heaven. Blessed are they that mourn: for they shall be comforted. Blessed are the meek: for they shall inherit the earth. Blessed are they which do hunger and thirst after righteousness: for they shall be filled. Blessed are the merciful: for they shall obtain mercy. Blessed are the pure in heart: for they shall see God. Blessed are the peacemakers: for they shall be called the children of God. Blessed are they which are persecuted for righteousness' sake: for theirs is the kingdom of heaven. Blessed are ye, when men shall revile you, and persecute you, and shall say all manner of evil against you falsely, for my sake. Rejoice, and be exceeding glad; for great is your reward in heaven: for so persecuted they the prophets which were before you.

"Ye are the salt of the earth: but if the salt have lost his savour, wherewith shall it be salted? It is thenceforth good for nothing, but to be cast out, and to be trodden under foot of men. Ye are the light of the world. A city that is set on an hill cannot be hid. Neither do men light a candle, and put it under a bushel, but on a candlestick; and it giveth light unto all that are in the house. Let your light so shine before men, that they may see your good works, and glorify your Father which is in heaven.

"Think not that I am come to destroy the law, or the prophets: I am not come to destroy, but to fulfil. For verily I say unto you, Till heaven and earth pass, one jot or one tittle shall in no wise pass from the law, till all be fulfilled. Whosoever therefore shall break one of these least commandments, and shall teach men so, he shall be called the least in the kingdom of heaven: but whosoever shall do and teach them, the same shall be called great in the kingdom of heaven. For I say unto you, That except your righteousness shall exceed the righteousness of the scribes and Pharisees, ye shall in no case enter into the kingdom of heaven.

"Ye have heard that it was said by them of old time, Thou shalt not kill; and whosoever shall kill shall be in danger of the judgment: But I say unto you, That whosoever is angry with his brother without a cause shall be in danger of the judgment: and whosoever shall say to his brother, Raca, shall be in danger of the council: but whosoever shall say, Thou fool, shall be in danger of hell fire. Therefore if thou bring thy gift to the altar, and there rememberest that thy brother hath aught against thee; leave there thy gift before the altar, and go thy way; first be reconciled to thy brother, and then come and offer thy gift. Agree with thine adversary quickly, whiles thou art in the way with him; lest at any time the adversary deliver thee to the judge, and the judge deliver thee to the officer, and thou be cast into prison. Verily I say unto thee, Thou shalt by no means come out thence, till thou hast paid the uttermost farthing.

"Ye have heard that it was said by them of old

time, Thou shall not commit adultery: But I say unto you, That whosoever looketh on a woman to lust after her hath committed adultery with her already in his heart. And if thy right eye offend thee, pluck it out, and cast it from thee: for it is profitable for thee that one of thy members should perish, and not that thy whole body should be cast into hell. And if thy right hand offend thee, cut it off, and cast it from thee: for it is profitable for thee that one of thy members should perish, and not that thy whole body should be cast into hell. It hath been said, Whosoever shall put away his wife, let him give her a writing of divorcement: But I say unto you, That whosoever shall put away his wife, saving for the cause of fornication, causeth her to commit adultery: and whosoever shall marry her that is divorced committeth adultery.

"Again, ye have heard that it hath been said by them of old time, Thou shalt not forswear thyself, but shalt perform unto the Lord thine oaths: But I say unto you, Swear not at all; neither by heaven; for it is God's throne: Nor by the earth; for it is his footstool: neither by Jerusalem; for it is the city of the great King. Neither shalt thou swear by thy head, because thou canst not make one hair white or black. But let your communication be, Yea, yea; Nay, nay: for whatever is more than these cometh of evil.

"Ye have heard that it hath been said, An eye for an eye, and a tooth for a tooth: But I say unto you, That ye resist not evil: but whosoever shall smite thee on thy right cheek, turn to him the other also. And if any man will sue thee at the law, and take away thy coat, let him have thy cloak also. And Whosoever shall compel thee to go a mile, go with him twain. Give to him that asketh thee, and from him that would borrow of thee turn not thou away.

"Ye have heard that it hath been said, Thou shalt love thy neighbour, and hate thine enemy. But I say unto you, Love your enemies, bless them that curse you, do good to them that hate you, and pray for them which despitefully use you, and persecute you; that ye may be the children of your Father which is in heaven: for he maketh his sun to rise on the evil and on the good, and sendeth rain on the just and the unjust. For if ye love them which love you, what reward have ye? do not even the publicans the same? And if ye salute your brethren only, what do ye more than others? do not even the publicans so? Be ye therefore perfect, even as your Father which is in heaven is perfect.

"Well, so much for the reading. I have found it valuable in sharing this with friends to whom I was seeking to witness. Sometimes as I go to preach, I've read this in the worship services. It has always been well received by the believers. Some of the churches have requested copies. They read a portion in the services of worship. I hope that it achieves a wider circulation.

"You know, Simon, I was the most unpromising and unlikely material for a disciple. If Jesus could call me and use me, a lowly publican, he can certainly save anyone! Well, the hour is late and I can see you are tired by my reading. Let us go to bed. Good night, old friend."

5
Peter, Apostle Extraordinary
John 6:66-69

The year is AD 61. Simon Peter is preaching to Christians in the catacombs outside the city of Rome.

"My little children and followers in the Way, I am pleased to see you here and to share with you the gospel news concerning Jesus of Nazareth who is Lord and Savior.

"I know most of you have labored long and hard today. Those of you who are slaves, remember we are one in Christ. Those of you who are masters, remember you have a Master in heaven. I will not keep you late. It is dark here, and the burning of your oil lamps makes the air heavy.

"I want to thank you for the warm welcome you have given John Mark and me. This young friend is a true follower in the Way. He journeyed with me from Jerusalem. He has been a constant source of help and encouragement. His dear mother is a great daughter of Israel. It was in the upper room of her home that we ate the last Passover with Jesus and he instituted what we have come to call the Lord's Supper.

"John Mark has been setting down on parchment an account of Jesus' life and teachings gleaned from my teaching and remembrances. He and others have a growing concern that we apostles are falling prey to the enemies of the faith. (Indeed, I understand that Paul is chained to a Roman soldier in prison here in Rome.) John Mark's idea is that a permanent account should be recorded which can outlive the apostles.

"Please hold your lamps so the light falls on your faces. When I preach, it helps if I can look into your eyes. There is so much I want to share with you. I feel as though my heart would burst, and the time is short.

"Tonight let me share the account of three mornings with the Master.

"My home in Galilee is nothing like your imperial city with its forum, triumphal arches, palaces, baths, and seven hills. By contrast I am afraid that Galilee is quite provincial. The sleepy fishing village of Capernaum is at the head of the Sea of Galilee which is really an inland lake by comparison to the Great Sea. We have only one grand building. It is a synagogue built by the Roman soldier whose son Jesus healed, but that's another story. That's the trouble with old preachers—every story recalls another. It's like unraveling a sleeve.

"I followed my father's trade and inherited his fishing boats, nets, and business. Most of my neighbors were fishermen too. Not that we were really bitter competitors. There were always plenty of fish and a ready market in the booming Roman cities of Tiberis and Caesarea. We usually fished by night with torches to attract the fish into our nets.

"Fishermen are at one and the same time a pious and a rowdy lot. Anyone who depends on the sea for his livelihood must learn to pray. However, the work is hard with the heat and reflecting torches. Fishermen can be profane—swearing and praying! James, the pastor in Jerusalem, once nailed me on that. He said, 'Simon, why is it a man with the same tongue blesses God and curses man who is made in God's image?' All I could do was agree that it shouldn't be so.

"First, let me tell you of the morning I met the Master. We had heard of this new rabbi from across the Mount Carmel range at Nazareth. He was traveling in our area of Galilee teaching and healing. Some of my neighbors heard him. They were simply ecstatic. 'He doesn't talk like other men. He speaks with such authority, never quoting the rabbis, but he always speaks in such a straightforward fashion.' Jesus' directness appealed to people. He would begin by saying, 'I say to you.' Dry speakers who repeat others' words may impress some learned scholar, but they seldom ring the bells in a common man's heart. They produce few wet cheeks or changed lives.

"We heard rumors of his healing power. 'Old wives tales,' said I. 'I'll get my sleep. You won't find me traipsing off to hear every new preacher or pseudomessiah.'

"I sat crouching on my haunches repairing my nets. My brother, Andrew, came up breathlessly, 'Oh, Simon, we have found the Messiah.' I mumbled something about how that wasn't going to fix my blasted nets. Suddenly, out of the corner of my sleepless eye, I caught sight of a long shadow. Looking up and squinting into the sun, I could see a man the like of which I had never seen before.

"He was tall and muscular with the rough hands of a carpenter. His eyes were deeply set and piercing. One felt as though one's soul was naked before him. Then I heard his strong yet soft voice, 'Simon, come follow me, and I will make you a fisher of men.' I felt compelled, drawn by this magnetic figure. I forgot the nets and even the clink of the silver which they would bring. I left my business in the care of a neighbor and joined Jesus. His teaching and his miraculous healings blessed my soul. Surely, all I had heard about him must be true. This must surely be the Messiah!

"For the next three years we followed him. I told you when last we met, about the last week he spent on this earth. It began with his triumphal entry into Jerusalem to the praise of the crowd. Arguments by his enemies erupted that week. Then there was that night, that unforgettable night in the upper room. We had entered such rivals to be rebuked by Jesus washing our feet. I told you about the eating of the Passover and the institution of the Lord's Supper and about our sleeping in Gethsemane while he prayed. You will also remember the account of my denial of the Lord. I always tell that wherever I go. My denial of Jesus was the most terrible experience of my life and yet one of the grandest illustrations of the matchless grace of God. You see, if Jesus could forgive me, he can forgive anyone.

"But you are yawning. It is late. I am sure you are

weary, and the oil in your lamps is burning low. The second account must be brief.

"It was Sunday morning after the awful experience of my denial and Jesus' crucifixion. I awoke to the sound of fists pounding on the door. My hand went for the sword underneath my pillow, and I looked for a window where I might escape. After all, the authorities had put Jesus to death. Being one of his disciples, I might very well share his fate.

"As I came somewhat more awake, it dawned on me that the voices outside were women's voices. They were talking all at once in frantic confusion. I opened the door and Mary Magdalene spoke for the group. She had been to the tomb and found it empty. She was saying something about the Lord being risen from the dead. She said she had seen the risen Lord, and he had given her instructions to go and tell his disciples and Peter. Can you imagine? Risen? 'Tell my disciples and Peter?' I tell you the truth, if he had not added the words, 'and Peter,' I would not have counted myself any longer his disciple or worthy to seek him.

"I reached for my cloak, dressing hurriedly. John, who was sleeping in the next room, was awake by then. The two of us ran out into the street and hurried along to the garden tomb. The women followed, continuing to tell what happened. When it seemed as though we had the gist of their story, we broke away from them and began to run toward the tomb. We found the soldiers gone. The huge stone had been rolled back in its slot from the entrance. The morning sun was beaming through the doorway.

John, being younger and slimmer than I, outran me and arrived first at the tomb. He stood looking in. On reaching the site, I rushed into the open tomb. There I saw the clothes in which Jesus had been buried and the napkin folded neatly. However, he was not there. In a flash, it came to us. Had he not said, 'I will be seized and killed and on the third day I will rise from the dead?' It was true! Impossible, unbelievable, yet true. He was risen from the dead!

"The third morning with the Master was one in Galilee. It was not unlike the first in which I initially met Jesus.

"After witnessing the empty tomb and knowing that surely something marvelous had happened, I said to the others in the disciple band, 'Let's return to Galilee, for according to the women's account, he promised to meet us there.' As we reached our old haunts, I said to the others, 'I'm going fishing.' It was like old times that night, except that we seemed almost haunted by the memory of the risen Christ.

"About dawn, as our boat was nearing the shore, we saw the figure of a man standing beside a charcoal fire with the smoke circling above his head. This was not an unusual sight around this area at all. It was then that John, with his unusual perception, said, 'It is the Lord!' We turned the boat toward shore, and the slight wind began to fill the sail. However, my heart beat within me as though it would burst out of my chest. I couldn't wait for the slow boat to reach the shore. I plunged headlong into the sea, swimming and wading toward the figure on the bank. When we met, neither of us said a word.

"On the fire there was fish and fried bread. Our breakfast being prepared, we ate in silence.

"Then it was that he drew me aside. He put his question to me quietly and yet with the certain skill of a master teacher.

"'Simon, do you love me?'

"With assurance I replied, 'Yes, Lord, I love you.'

"Then he said, 'Feed my sheep.' His question was repeated a second time, and I gave the same answer, and then a third time.

"'Simon, do you really love me?'

"To which I responded, 'Yes, Lord, you know all things. You know that I love you.'

"To this he gave the same answer, 'Feed my sheep.'

"Then it dawned on me. Three times I had denied him; three times he had asked my love.

"Brethren, this is what I am about, feeding his sheep, caring for the flock of God. This has been my task since that third morning in Galilee and shall be my task until I die.

"As I entered your city, it seemed as though I met the Master once again. My question to him was, *'Quo vadis?'* (Where are you going?). Wherever he goes, I shall follow. Whatever he requires, I shall give, even if it means my life.

"Perhaps that's the question for you to answer: *Quo vadis?* Let me invite you to go with the Master."

6
John, Son of Thunder
Matthew 4:18-22; Mark 3:17

Wouldn't you like to have known the apostles in person? Suppose you could go back to the year AD 96. You are at the home of Alexander, the Greek pastor of the church in Ephesus, in Asia Minor. You are listening to the aged apostle John as he talks with Alexander. The two men, one not thirty and the other past ninety, are sitting in an open courtyard. There are lovely spring flowers all about, and the air is filled with their fragrance and the sound of birds singing. The two sit soaking up the warm morning sun. Listen as John speaks, haltingly at first and then more clearly as he warms to his narration.

"Alexander, my young brother, you have been so kind to me. You and your dear people practice the Christian virtue of hospitality most graciously. I am in your debt. You've taken this old man in as though I were your father. Indeed, I do feel a fatherly affection for you and your congregation. They have been kind to me. They say I appear twenty years younger than I am. Age is a strange thing. It becomes the old man's badge of distinction. Suddenly, we don't feel complimented when we are taken to be younger than we are. I suppose that's all part of our human vanity. But here I am chattering about nonessentials when I want to take this morning with you to tell you some important visions I haven't discussed with anyone yet. I want to tell you what a difference Jesus has made in my life, and I want you to understand my divine compulsion to share the most encouraging words Christians can read today. I also want you to understand what I've recently experienced and to commit it to writing so the churches can circulate copies and read it in their assemblies. The churches here in Asia, and beyond, must hear the risen Christ's message.

"My recent exile on Patmos in the Aegean Sea was no friend to age. The constant dampness and my meager living conditions in that island cave took their toll on my health. It has grown fragile, I fear. When Emperor Domitian was murdered last fall, the senate in Rome repealed his oppressive laws and freed all political prisoners. You can't imagine the ecstatic joy I felt at my release.

"I shall always recall with joy your congregation's grand welcome. They were so excited at my release. They made my homecoming a thing of beauty. I recall that they packed the meeting place here in your courtyard. I was so weak from my ordeal that I had to be helped into the meeting by two of your deacons, Rufus and Tychicus. Tychicus is the brother who brought the letter from missionary Paul to Ephesus. Though you were away at the time, you have every reason to feel a pastor's pride in your people. I was so weak that I could not preach. While the men supported me, I kept saying to your dear people, 'Little

children, love one another. Little children, love one
another.'

"The privation on Patmos was not the worst of it,
Alexander. The hardest thing was the separation. To
be called to preach the good news and then be shut
away from people is torture. One of the glorious
things I saw in my vision of the Holy City is that there
is no more sea there—no more separation! Indeed,
that will be glory! We will be with him, and with our
beloved who are in Christ. But more about that later.

"My, that warm goat's milk was good! That,
added to this sun, will warm these old bones inside
and out. Helen is a fine cook. You were fortunate in
many ways in the happy choice of a wife. No one is
more important in a man's ministry than his companion of the way. Excuse me, I'm rambling again.

"To come to the point, Alexander, while I was on
Patmos I had a number of visions. I've come to see
what the last days will be like, and I've heard a series
of messages from the risen Christ to the churches of
the province of Asia. In a vision on the Lord's Day, I
heard a voice which said, 'I am Alpha and Omega,
who is and who was, and who is coming, the Almighty.' Then I heard the voice behind me, loud as a
trumpet call, command me to write down in a book
what I saw and to send it to the seven churches—to
Ephesus, Smyrna, Pergamum, Thyatira, Sardis, Philadelphia, and Laodicea.

"I turned to see who was speaking to me, and I
saw seven golden lampstands. Among them I saw
someone like the Son of man. He was dressed in a

long robe with a golden belt around his waist, his hair was snow-white, his eyes blazed like fire, and his feet shone as the finest bronze glows in the furnace. His voice sounded like the roar of a great waterfall. In his right hand he held seven stars. A sharp two-edged sword came out of his mouth, and his face was shining like the sun at its height. When my eyes took in this sight, I fell at his feet. He placed his right hand on me and said,

"'Do not be afraid. I am the first and the last, the Living One. I am he who was dead, and now you see me alive for endless ages! I hold in my hand the keys of death and the grave. I am victor over them. Therefore, write what you have seen, both the things which are now and the things which are to be hereafter. The seven stars in my right hand and the seven golden lampstands represent the seven churches.'

"Then the Christ gave me a message for each of the churches, including yours here in Ephesus. I have written down the messages to the churches. I will need your help and that of the church to have copies made for circulation among them. Each church should profit by hearing the messages to the others, as well as the one designated for itself. Perhaps churches in other areas will also want copies.

"Alexander, I saw more on Patmos. I was given a glimpse at the last page of human history. I have been privileged to see what will be hereafter and it spells victory, victory, victory—victory for good, victory for God, and victory for the gospel! I've determined, dear brother, to write a Christian apocalypse—a veiled message. It will be in a sort of code. It will contain both literal and symbolic elements. In this way it will be unintelligible to the Roman authorities should it fall into their hands. Yet it will be intelligible and meaningful to believers who are familiar with Jewish apocalyptic literature such as the Book of Daniel's prophecy. My purpose in writing his revelation is to encourage persecuted believers. The risen Lord commanded me to write the message for their benefit. Great and terrible things are about to come upon the church, Alexander. I want to say to them, *'Sursum Corda'*—lift up your hearts!

"It has been six years now since I completed my gospel account and my three short letters to the churches. The messages to the seven churches of Asia and the apocalypse will complete my ministry of writing. Alexander, my young brother, should I climb the martyr's steep ascent to glory before the apocalypse is complete, will you finish it for me, on the basis of what I relate to you? Thank you! Thank you! I am anxious that this important message not be left incomplete. I do feel that it can encourage the churches till the Lord comes.

"You know I was the youngest of the twelve, and as far as I know I may be the last alive. My brother James was the first of us to die. He met his death at the command of Herod whom our Lord once called, 'that old fox.' Andrew was slain in Greece across the Aegean. Thomas went far to the east as messenger of the good news, and we haven't heard from him in years. There were earlier reports of his success in planting the gospel there. When I returned from

Patmos, I was saddened to learn that both Simon Peter and missionary Paul have died in Rome—Peter by crucifixion and Paul by decapitation. I fear, Alexander, that the fate befalling the church's leaders will soon come upon the church as a whole. Demonic powers will not take the church's success lying down. While I'm no pessimist, it's all too clear that days of testing are at hand. As for me, in the words of Paul's last letter, 'the time of my departure is at hand, and I am ready to be offered,' poured in sacrifice, if it so pleases the Lord God.

"My, but the smell of that fish being smoked reminds me of days in Galilee! They seem so long ago and far away. You know, of course, that my brother James, my father Zebedee, and I were fishermen on the Sea of Galilee (which the Romans call Lake Tiberias). Our mother, Salome, was a sister of Mary of Nazareth, Jesus' mother. These crow's feet came around my eyes from squinting into the bright sun reflecting off the water there. The truth is I was never a very good fisherman. As long as the lake's waters were calm, I was all right. But when there was the least storm (and there were often violent ones), I was the first man to get seasick. I'd lose my toes! I remember how impatient my brother would get with me, for my work was added to his in hauling in the nets and rowing.

"I shall never forget the call of Jesus to be his disciple. It wasn't just an impulsive decision. We had heard our cousin from Nazareth preach a number of times in Galilee—at Nazareth (wow, that was a service to remember!) and at Capernaum. Even before the beginning of Jesus' ministry, James and I had become disciples of John the Baptist. It was the imprisonment of John, of course, that signaled the beginning of Jesus' ministry. He called us that day from mending our nets. His words were graphic, 'You are fishers. I will make you fishers of men.' He later told us that he called us to be with him and that he might send us forth to preach the good news of the kingdom. After his death, resurrection, and ascension, his ministry was committed to us and through the twelve to speak to men like you. So the message will continue to spread until he returns.

"I'd like to tell you many things about those days with the Master. But time will not allow, and I've set much of it down, along with my studied reflection, in my Gospel account.

"Do let me tell you about Jesus' nickname for James and me. He called us, 'sons of thunder.' It was not a highly complimentary handle, but an accurate one I'm afraid. You see, we were a highly ambitious pair, and, on top of that, our mother, Salome, was ambitious for us. I suppose every mother wants to see her boys do well and make a place for themselves in life. We shared our excitement about Jesus and the kingdom with her. One day she went with us to talk with the Master. We tried to get a commitment from him to grant our request before we stated it. The request was that we be named his first and second ministers or cabinet members once he established the kingdom.

"Our request was not so unreasonable as it might sound on the surface. For one thing, the disciple band was a rather ragtag group. Most of the twelve were men of very common means. James and I were from a fairly well-to-do family. Our father, Zebedee, owned a fishing fleet, and he had hired servants who carried on the business after James and I went to full-time religious work. Further, our father had contributed financially to the support of Jesus' work. All this was due some consideration we felt. Still further, there was the matter of our kinship with the Master— which is no small matter in the East. After all, blood is thicker than water, you know. We felt that our joint request for preference was quite in order.

"I remember Jesus' gentle rebuke. He said, 'You don't know what you ask.' And as it turned out, we really didn't understand that his kingdom was to be a spiritual and not a military one. Jesus went on to say, 'He who would be greatest in the kingdom must be servant of all.' That was a reversal of the world's standards and frankly, it was puzzling to us for a long time. Only in later years did we come to see what he meant. I'm sure Jesus' standard is one that many Christians will find hard to meet—yet it is essential for true discipleship.

"Another reason the Master called us 'sons of thunder' was that we had quick tempers. I recall an occasion when we were en route from Galilee to Jerusalem. There seemed an urgency in Jesus' manner, and we took the shortest way, going through Samaria. He sent the two of us on ahead of the party to arrange lodging for the night. Since James and I were the youngest of the twelve, we often drew such assignments. The Samaritans were plainly rude and refused us lodging. It was a simple case of racial and religious prejudice on their part. Prejudice is an ugly thing, Alexander, especially when you are its victim! We were outraged! We hurried back to Jesus and the band. 'Master,' we asked, 'shall we call down fire from heaven and destroy these inhospitable people?'

"'No,' said Jesus. And we went on to another village.

"It was ironic, Alexander, that after Pentecost deacon Philip was led by the Spirit to preach in Samaria. His words met with a ready and sympathetic response. Large crowds heard him, miracles were performed, and many came to believe in Jesus as Lord. The apostles and church in Jerusalem heard that Samaria had accepted the word of God. They sent Peter and me down to Samaria to verify these reports. We found that indeed they had become believers and had been baptized by Philip in the name of the Lord Jesus. We laid hands on the new converts, and they received the Holy Spirit. It was much like the experience of the believers here in Ephesus when Paul came on his first visit. You will recall how the dozen believers had been baptized with John's baptism and hadn't heard of the Holy Spirit! There was an episode with Simon, the magician, in Samaria, but that's another story. The point is that where I had once wanted to call down lightning to destroy people, I later prayed down the fire of the Holy Spirit on them! How different is the pleasure of God!

"There were other occasions that earned our nickname, 'sons of thunder.' Once we came upon a fellow who was healing the sick in Jesus' name. When we checked him out, we learned that he did not even belong to our disciple group—so we forbade him to heal in Jesus' name. After all, he wasn't one of us. That night at dinner I bragged to Jesus about what we'd done. Much to my surprise, Jesus said, 'Forbid him not. He that is not against us is for us.' I learned that the Jesus movement is bigger than I'd thought.

"It is true that James and I, along with Peter, were members of the inner circle within the disciple band. Only the three of us were present with Jesus at the raising of Jairus' daughter. We three were also the only ones present at the transfiguration of Jesus. We saw him glorified and heard him talk with Moses and Elijah on the mountaintop. I recall how Peter wanted to stay up there. Well, the truth is, we all did. It was so marvelous, much like my visions on Patmos.

"We three were also present with Jesus at his time of agony in Gethsemane, though we weren't much comfort to him. We were all bone-weary from the week's controversy and hostility. However, as you know, worse agony, much worse, was to come.

"Alexander, I do hope I have opportunity to tell you about the events of that last week. I was at the table with the Master in the upper room of John Mark's mother's house at Passover. I'll never forget how I felt when he said, 'One of you shall betray me.' That was an awesome time of heart searching, I'll tell you!

"I was present at Jesus' crucifixion and heard him say, 'Behold, your mother.' As you know, I cared for Mary until her death, here in Ephesus.

"I was the first of the twelve to arrive at the empty tomb on that first Easter morning. I outran old stubby-legged Peter. But brash fellow that he always was, he was the first to enter the tomb and verify that Jesus' body was indeed not there.

"Well, Alexander, as you can see, I'm an old man, and I'm prone to ramble on endlessly.

"Do let me say this, my young brother. Believers in the Christ need not fear death. I've had a glimpse of glory. It is absolutely indescribable! I intend to try to describe my vision of heaven in the apocalypse—with the most extravagant language at my command. But my poor words will prove as inadequate as trying to explain to an unborn child the beauty of a sunset or the fragrance of a rose!

"Alexander, my message to the young church is, 'Love one another.' That's the heart of our faith.

"What? What's that? How did a son of thunder become the beloved disciple? Oh, that's an easy one to answer. You see Jesus called us to be with him. You can't be with him very long and remain the same. Living in his presence is life-transforming.

"Remember, Alexander, tell your people: 'Love one another! Love one another!'"

7
James—An Autumn Bloom
1 Corinthians 15:3-8

Today we will go back to Jerusalem in the year AD 62 shortly before the martyrdom of the apostle James. We listen in on a conversation between James and young Timothy.

"Welcome, young friend, to Jerusalem the golden! It is a lovely time of the year to be here—the flowers are unusually beautiful this fall. However, the Holy City is crowded with pilgrims, come to celebrate Yom Kippur, our Day of Atonement. It is the most notable holy day among the Jewish people.

"I've been thrilled at your account of the apostle Paul and his missionary journeys through Asia Minor. It is marvelous, the response you've been having in evangelizing the Gentiles. How we rejoice that the faith is universal in its scope and not simply a sect within Judaism.

"As Paul may have told you, the church made the decision here at the Jerusalem Conference that determined the taking of the gospel to the Gentiles.

"I met Paul about three years after his conversion. This was following his stay in Arabia. He came to Jerusalem and conferred with Simon Peter and me. How we rejoiced that this persecutor had been won to the faith. He was held in suspicion, quite frankly, among many of the brethren. 'A Pharisee trick!' they suspected. However, Peter and I got to know him and taste his spirit. We were convinced of his sincerity. You know his intensity of concern and devotion to the cause, for you've traveled with him, as his most trusted colaborer. I know something of the bond of affection with which you regard your 'Father in the faith.' It is not ill-deserved I assure you, and you are to be commended for your loyalty to him.

"It was, I suppose, fourteen years later when I saw Paul next. The brethren had been called to the Jerusalem Conference to decide this matter of precisely how one becomes a believer. Some of us with our Jewish heritage felt that all Christians should keep the Jewish law. Paul, the Apostle to the Gentiles, broadened our view, to be perfectly frank. He told of the conversion of many of the Gentiles, how they had received the Holy Spirit, and how faithful they were in their devotion. I saw the wisdom of recognizing all believers and made a speech in favor of Paul's position. When the ballots were cast, the decision was unanimous. We were quite convinced that the Holy Spirit had led us.

"Paul and I are apostles though we were not among the twelve. He is the Apostle of the Gentiles, and I've been pastor of the church here in Jerusalem for nearly thirty years now. However, the political situation currently is flirting with disaster. Zealots are pushing our people too far, and one day Rome will overreact and destroy our nation, I fear. Religious hostility from the Jewish authorities is also building to a peak. We may soon be forced to climb the 'martyr's steep ascent to glory.'

"Say, Timothy, I'm intrigued and complimented at what you told me about the little epistle I wrote. I have a carpenter's education. This hardly equips me to be a scholar. However, I understand that my sermon on faith and work has been translated from Aramaic into Greek and is being circulated among the churches. I'm honored. However, it is a bit unfair to hear or read one sermon and judge a man by that. In a given message, one must emphasize only one point—just as good works is the emphasis in that sermon. In preaching it is difficult to give balance in a single message. This usually requires a series of sermons.

"Prayer has always been my favorite theme. I'm convinced that our spiritual poverty has a simple explanation—we have not because we ask not. God is gracious and anxious to bless, not reluctant. Our Lord taught that in several of his parables. The prayer of a righteous man accomplishes a great deal. I've found this to be very true in life. In recent years, I've made much of intercessory prayer. Ironically, this accounts for my nickname as old 'Camel Knees.'

"Jesus was a toddler when I was born. I suppose he was about two years of age. He was my big brother and helped care for me and our other brothers, Joses, Simon, and Judas—as well as our sisters. We grew up as boys together. We ate on the same bench and slept on the same pallet. We rambled the hills together during the afternoons. Those were carefree days. We both helped in the shop, cleaning up the shavings and running errands. There we learned Joseph's trade as carpenter.

"I recall that my older brother, Jesus, had quite a knack for storytelling. He would entertain us for hours on end with the glories of the history of our nation. We loved him dearly; and yet, at times, somehow I hardly know how to express it, he was different. I remember the days in the synagogue school. Only boys attended. I can remember that we worshiped with the family in the synagogue regularly. He sometimes would take part in reciting the Scriptures. However, Nazareth, where we grew up, was a little town. Life there was hard. It is a scenic place overlooking the plain of Esdraelon. On many a warm afternoon, we would sit and watch the caravans cross the plain like a distant trail of ants.

"Joseph died. He was older than our mother. Since Jesus was the eldest son, he became the head of the household. I became his junior partner in the cabinet shop. Business was good, even if taxes were oppressive. He had very high standards for our work, both for the material we used and for our workmanship.

"In time, I developed a reputation for honesty and fairness. My nickname became James the Just. One day Jesus hung up his apron, and the full weight of the business enterprise fell on me. My older brother became a traveling rabbi. I thought him not really qualified or trained to do that. Further, it left too much responsibility on me. I must confess that it caused me to delay my marriage for two years. However, to my surprise, his ministry was not a flop. Indeed, his reputation spread rapidly, and he was quite successful. His name was on all lips.

"He came home on occasion. There were times when he would slip into town to see my mother and the younger children. He was kind, but seemed preoccupied. Mother was very proud of him, of course. One sabbath when he was home, he was chosen preacher for the day at the synagogue. I felt he was unwise in his choice of text. He raised the racial question, saying that Elijah had been entertained by a pagan and leperous Naaman had been healed, though he was not a son of Abraham. His sympathies were far too broad for the citizens of Nazareth. He was no longer welcome in his hometown.

"Word spread that people were calling him the Messiah. Surely, he and they must be mad! I remember how my palms would sweat and embarrass me when I first heard the report. Quite frankly, it hurt business. My brothers and I did not believe that Jesus was the Messiah. I remember the stinging report when he was quoted as having said, 'A man's foes are in his own household.' Rumors continued to multiply of wonders and miracles he was working. We were afraid this would bring trouble from the authorities. Finally, I called a family council. We decided that our elder brother must be mad and that it was our duty as his brothers to bring him home. With Mary and my three brothers, we went to Capernaum and found the house where he was. There was a mob gathered outside. I sent in word. 'Tell him his mother and his brothers are here.' When the fellow to whom I had spoken came back, I asked, 'Is he coming?' He said simply, 'No.' 'Well, what did he say?' He said, 'My mother and my brothers are those who do the will of God.' 'Well, don't we? Well, at least we tried to bring him home.'

"I shall never forget when the end came. Word reached us that he was in trouble with the authorities in Jerusalem and then the horrible news that he had been crucified! We'd seen crosses in Galilee and knew what they were like. A thousand wonderful memories of earlier days flooded my mind and frankly, broke my heart. I remembered youth's bright morning. How tender and patient he had been. Such a dreamer he was, and now his dream was forever shattered. It dawned on me that I had lived in the midst of unrecognized greatness. I had lived with him for twenty-eight years and still did not really believe in his greatness.

"Then it happened! It was near the close of the business day. I was standing in the shop. The sun was setting toward the Mediterranean Sea. My heart was brimming full. I heard someone call my name. His voice was all too familiar. 'James, it is I.' I wheeled around to exclaim, 'Jesus.' It was true. My next word was, 'Messiah'! My wintry heart burst into spring. I can't tell you all he said then. Some of it so deep and intimate that it is simply impossible to share. The point is that I became a believer, and I did not stop until I had won our three brothers to faith in Jesus as the Christ.

"I guess you could say I'm an autumn bloom, for I had a late start. Timothy, remember what he said, 'My mother and my brothers are those who do the will of God.'"

8
The Distant Disciple—
Nicodemus
John 3:12-16; 7:45-53; 19:38-42

"Shalom! Let me introduce myself. I am a member of an old family in Jerusalem. We can trace our lineage back to the time when our nation returned from the Exile in Babylon. My family was prominent, especially during the time of Maccabean rule.

"As a guardian of the establishment, I belong to an elite religious sect within Judaism. We call ourselves Pharisees, or the 'separated ones.' We are a strict brotherhood made up of the best men of our people and pledged to obey the law and uphold the traditions of our fathers. We consider ourselves to be the true Israelites. We believe in the resurrection of the dead and look forward to the coming of the Messiah. My brothers expect him to be a militant figure who will drive the Romans from our holy city.

"Because of my position in the community, I am also on the seventy-member Jewish supreme court, the Sanhedrin. The Roman governor allows us considerable jurisdiction over the internal government of the province. Our religious authority extends to every Jewish male in the world. The high priest himself is our president or chief justice. My membership in this body marks me as a ruler of the Jews.

"I have quite a reputation as a rabbi or teacher among my people. Some give me the title, 'The Teacher.' My chief teacher was Gamaliel, of whom you may have heard!

"Modesty has never been exactly a virtue among my brotherhood. Therefore, allow me to say that I represent the quintessence of Judaism, or the Jewish faith.

"I have always considered myself a practical, rational man. I pride myself on being not only a good and obedient son of Abraham but also a fair one. Above everything else, a ruler must be fair!

"At Passover some five springs ago, we had quite a stir in the capital. An intense young rabbi from Galilee came to the feast accompanied by a group of his students or disciples. He caused quite a ruckus by driving the sellers of sacrificial animals and birds out of the Temple complex—with a plaited whip! He also upset the tables of the money changers. It very nearly precipitated a riot. The high priest was livid! He had licensed the stalls and received a handsome commission on their profits.

"However, what really upset my party, the Pharisees, was what this fellow Jesus said as he cleared the place out. 'You shall not make my Father's house a house of trade!'

"His Father's house, indeed. Who did he think he was? That was what my fellow Pharisees wanted to know. Then it was reported that he said he would destroy the Temple and rebuild it in three days. An absurd claim, we thought.

"My group was up in arms against this fellow

Jesus. 'But let us be fair,' I said. 'Let's examine all the facts.' Jesus did a number of miracles, or signs, as he called them. I didn't put much stock in them until my blind cousin was healed by him. It was an authentic miracle. From that moment, I knew we must take this rabbi seriously. Our writings say that if a prophet gives a sign or a miracle he is to be listened to.

"Let me confess that despite my family's wealth and my own prominence as a rabbi in Jerusalem, something was lacking to me. I have kept the law all my adult life. Yet there was little joy in it all. It was largely an external affair of ritual cleanliness and righteousness. At a deeper level I had been a seeker after truth for some time before I met the Master. I certainly had a veneer of respectability, but underneath I felt a nagging void. I determined to meet Jesus and examine his claims and teachings for myself. After all, it was the only fair thing to do.

"I decided to arrange an interview with Jesus. I had to go by night. There were several reasons for this. Night was the favorite time for rabbis to discuss the law and theology among themselves. It was a quiet time when there would be little likelihood of interruption. Further, the visit must be kept confidential. He was a highly controversial person. Discretion dictated that the interview be conducted privately.

"As I have thought about that interview since that night, I realize that I came to Jesus out of spiritual darkness as well.

"I shall never forget that warm spring evening. I had made arrangements with one of his disciples,

Andrew, for the interview. He met me at the door of the guest house and said his master was waiting for me on the flat roof. I climbed the outside stair with pounding heart. Why should a man of my position be so excited about meeting this humble Galilean? Maybe it was some deep longing inside me or perhaps some sort of premonition that tonight could be of eternal importance.

"I arrived at the roof to see him standing in the moonlight. He came forward to receive me. I expected him to be tired and bedraggled. Andrew had astutely indicated that he had been teaching and healing since daybreak. However, Jesus looked completely rested and composed; much more than I, after climbing the steps. Stairs were never my favorite invention. He looked so young! He couldn't have been more than thirty. His eyes were piercing, even by moonlight. His sharp intelligence fairly flashed from those clear eyes. He looked like a king!

"Once I'd caught my breath and regained my composure, I began the conversation politely.

"'Rabbi,' I said, 'we know that you are a teacher come from God; for no one can do these signs that you do, unless God is with him.' I approached him as one theologian to another, speaking for the Jewish religious establishment.

"His reply shocked me. He said, 'Amen, amen, I say to you, unless you are born again you cannot see the kingdom of God.' It was as though he was saying, 'Let's not talk about me and my miracles, but about you and your entry into the kingdom.' I had been diplomatic and complimentary. Jesus' reply ignored these tributes and went like a rapier to the heart of my own spiritual problem.

"I wasn't to be dealt with so abruptly. I took him quite literally and said, 'Born again? How can a man be born when he is old? Can he enter a second time into his mother's womb and be born?' My mind was whirling at the thought. The very idea! Proselytes to Judaism were said to be born again. But what need had a Hebrew to be born more than as a son of Abraham? Incredible! Once a man is old his habits and life patterns are fixed. He doesn't make such a radical change!

"Then Jesus said, 'Unless one is born of water and the Spirit, he cannot enter the kingdom of God.'

"'Born of water,' conjured up vivid memories of John the Baptist and his water baptism of good Jews! What an explosion that had set off among my Pharisee brethren!

"'Born of the Spirit.' Such a thing could take place only once the Messiah had come! What could he mean?

"Then Jesus pointed out the sovereignty of the warm night wind. 'The wind blows where it wills,' he said. Now do you suppose the divine will is all that spontaneous? We thought we had God shut up in the law and our culture, our worship. Could he be bringing new truth into our stuffy Temple on the fresh ideas of this young rabbi? I couldn't be precisely sure of his meaning. He used a play on words. You see, in our language the same word means breath, wind, or spirit. It took some thinking to unravel that one.

"'How can this be?' I asked.

"Jesus wanted to make it clear that he was not talking about human birth but about spiritual birth. He seemed disappointed that I was so slow to catch his meaning. 'Nicodemus,' he said, 'are you a teacher of Israel, and yet you do not understand this?'

"Then he said—and I can never forget the words—'For God so loved the world that he gave his only Son, that whoever believes in him should not perish but have eternal life.' I did not understand the full import of those words until later—much later!

"The antithesis of faith is not doubt, but unbelief. How hard it was for me to believe that this intense young Galilean could be the Son of God—the Messiah. The interview concluded with my being in a spiritual quandary. A battle was raging inside me. I wanted to believe, yet I had so much religious tradition to 'unlearn,' as it were. I wanted to uphold what I had always known, and I wanted to believe this radical new birth was possible for me as well. I had no peace of mind. I wanted to declare for him, but I had too much to give up. A prudent man is seldom at peace! That interview created a moral dilemma for me.

"It was not until the next year at the Feast of Tabernacles in Jerusalem that I saw Jesus again. The Sanhedrin decided to send certain persons to check him out. They reported to the Sanhedrin, 'No man ever spoke like this man!'

"The vast majority of the court was too blinded by prejudice against Jesus to be fair. They asked, 'Have any of the Pharisees believed in him? This rabble crowd, these people of the land are accursed!'

"My heart was in my throat. I wanted to say, 'Yes, this Pharisee believes in him!' But I didn't dare. That was not the time or the place. The fever of their opposition to Jesus was at too high a pitch.

"Mustering all my courage, I asked, 'Does our law judge a man without first giving him a hearing? Let's be fair!'

"But they turned on me almost to a man. 'Are you from Galilee too?' one member screamed. 'Search the Scriptures and you will see that no prophet comes from Galilee.' Only later did I learn that Jesus was born in Bethlehem of Judea! They didn't think any Galilean was ever to be taken seriously. Their contempt was something to behold. Prejudice is never uglier than when it is religious prejudice.

"I stood alone. Never before in all my life had I felt so alone. Little did I notice or suspect that my lame defense of Jesus had a telling effect on one of our Sanhedrin members. Joseph, from the northern Judean village of Arimathea, took in all I'd said. He was a good man who was looking for the kingdom of God. He was a new member of the council, in contrast to my old family. My defense of Jesus was enough to set Joseph thinking.

"The next Passover was a sheer nightmare. Jesus returned to Jerusalem in triumph to the praise of the common people. This only served to crystallize the religious authorities' opposition to him. They were determined to see him dead.

"An illegal meeting of the council was called in the early hours of Friday morning. 'Conveniently' the messenger did not get word to me. I suppose they thought I might stall for time. When I heard about the trial at midmorning, I was surprised to learn one white stone had been cast. There was one other member who believed Jesus was innocent! Nevertheless, Jesus was condemned to death.

"Shortly before noon, I went outside the city wall to the place of execution. It was incredible that such a magnificent life could be snuffed out. As I watched him hanging there, suddenly I recalled something he had said to me that night. 'As Moses lifted up the serpent in the wilderness, so must the Son of man be lifted up, that whoever believes in him may have eternal life.'

"Suddenly, I understood! I knew! It was true! Jesus is the Son of God! But how could it end like this—with a criminal's cross? I turned to flee. As I ran down the hill, I bumped into a hooded figure. Through tears, I made out the familiar face. It was Joseph of Arimathea! He was the one who had cast the white stone—the innocent vote.

"Joseph took me over to the west side of the hill. We went up a narrow walled street and through a gate. It opened onto a quiet, lovely garden. There Joseph showed me his newly hewn family tomb. Looking eastward, I could still see the silhouette of the three crosses.

"We made our plans quietly. Joseph would procure Jesus' body from Pilate. I would meet him at the garden tomb with linen and spices for the Master's burial. We went our separate ways.

"When I returned, carrying nearly a hundred

pounds of myrrh and aloes, I found Joseph there with his precious burden.

"Lovingly, we bathed the body, cleaning the wounds and the pierced brow. We laid his body on the white linen sheet and covered it. Then, pouring on the spices, we wrapped the body in winding cloths. It was a burial befitting a king—the King of the Jews. We had to work hurriedly, for the sabbath was at hand. What a scene we must have made—two secret disciples who came over to the Master's side only after his death! It is a sad, almost tragic note. We often leave our kindest tribute until it is too late.

"But there was a glory about it too. His death gave us courage. We forgot our fear. The Cross made the difference. It is the magnet that will one day draw all kinds of people to the Master.

"I believe. Jesus is the promised Messiah.

"He has changed my life. I have been born again—after I was old.

"What about you?"

9
Paul in Rome
Acts 28:30-31

Imagine yourself in Paul's rented house in Rome in AD 67. Paul is guarded by a Roman soldier named Brutus.

"Who? Who is it, Brutus? Timothy! Ah, yes, my son in the ministry, Timothy. I'm expecting him. Please have him come in.

"Welcome, Timothy, my boy. Welcome to the imperial city. You need not pay too much attention to Brutus, my Roman guard. He is a giant of a man, but his name is a misnomer. He is not really the brute he appears to be. He has a heart as big as he is, and the truth is he walks in 'the Way.'

"Oh, what a sight for sore eyes you are, Timothy. I'm so pleased you've come. I've been excited about it since I got word yesterday that you were en route.

"You've brought my cloak, which I left in Troas. Put it about my shoulders, if you will. I don't know whether as I get older I feel the cold more or whether Rome simply has a worse winter climate than my native Tarsus. It seems to me that winter comes a bit earlier each year and lingers.

"You've brought the scrolls and the manuscripts. Good! I've been anxious to do some further writing.

"Before you sit down and before the sun sets, look about you. From my rented house here, we can look directly down at the Roman forum. Rome on the Tiber is the hub of the empire, the center of the world! Isn't she an impressive city? What citizen would not feel pride at her splendor and greatness. In the forum you can see the toga-clad senators. Look there, to the left, see the Roman senate with its great, burnished bronze doors. The senate and the emperor have brought to the world the most efficient rule in its history. There to the west you see the Palatine hill with its grandiose palaces of the nobility. Beyond the forum is the Circus Maximus. What a city! It is *the* city in the world. Only Jerusalem moves me more.

"Timothy, I'm a child of the city. I grew up in Tarsus, which is no mean city. It is quite cosmopolitan. I've been privileged by God to plant churches in the city centers of the Roman empire. My sermon and writing illustrations have come from the city. I've used illustrations from the stadium, the theater, the market, the law courts, and triumphant processions. Unlike our Lord, who was himself a small townsman and countryman in his human life, I have been an urbanite.

"Rome has given us the *'Pax Romana,'* peace of Rome. They have brought law and order to our world. With their roads they have given us communication such as the world has never known before. They have cleared the sea of pirates and the highways of brigands. It's all worked out to the furtherance of the gospel, let me say.

"But Timothy, majestic Rome has a dark underside. At heart she is sick. For Rome is corrupt and immoral, without hope and without God in the world.

"These are crude and cruel days. Caesar Nero must surely be a mad man. He is exhausting the catalog of crimes! He poisoned his stepbrother, Britannicus. He kicked to death Poppaea, his second wife. He divorced, banished, and killed Octavia, his first wife. My son, I fear for the Christians in Rome. They could be made a ready scapegoat for some imperial mischief.

"Yet there are saints—even in Caesar's household. Believers march in the Roman legions. Three of my guards during the last two years have come to embrace 'the Way.' Among the oarsmen on imperial galleons, among the slaves who work the quarry, among the household servants who scurry about the imperial palace there are believers in the risen Christ.

"But enough of that. You look well, my boy. You are maturing, filling out a bit; but that baby face of yours will keep you looking young for years to come. I know the problems its brought you. The elders of the churches have tended to look down upon you because of your youth and not paid proper heed to your counsel. That's why I've always urged you to be a good student of the Scriptures.

"I've been gravely ill in recent days, but I am much better, thank you. I've been made to think recently that the time of my departure is at hand.

This is why your visit means so very much to me just now. I do not know what is ahead. It may be that I will soon climb the martyr's steep ascent to glory. Whatever comes, I know this—nothing can ever separate us from the love of God which is in Christ Jesus!

"For the past two years I've been living in my own rented house here in Rome. Of course, I am under house arrest. Soldiers guard me day and night. I can't go out to the catacombs or to any public meetings of believers. However, I am privileged to receive visitors here in my home and to write. Timothy, never neglect the ministry of the pen. The written word may be poor substitute for preaching, but it is a valuable tool. I've used it extensively in keeping up with and ministering to the churches I have established across the empire.

"Since I've been in Rome, I've had occasion to write a couple of letters. I've written to Philemon, returning Onesimus, his runaway slave. I admonished Philemon to receive Onesimus not any longer as a slave but as a beloved brother.

"That wonderful congregation in Philippi has done such a beautiful thing for me. They sent Epaphroditus here to Rome with a generous gift. That dear congregation is the only one which has contributed consistently to my missionary ministry. I've written them a letter trying to express my joy at the gracious thing they have done for me.

"What's that? How did I come to Rome? Oh, yes. It has slipped my mind that I have failed to write you concerning this. Let me go back a bit. When I was at Ephesus for three years, I carried on considerable correspondence. I wrote four different letters to the church in Corinth. They were so troubled by divisions and immorality in the congregation. One of my letters was a rather hot one, I am afraid. I thought better of it and wrote a reconciling letter later.

"While I was in Ephesus, I contracted malaria. That's such a swampy area. If something isn't done, the city one day will be no more! This malaria constituted a thorn or stake in my flesh. It affected my eyes, making it difficult for me to read or to stand the glare of sunlight.

"While there I wrote to the Christians in Rome, expressing my desire to preach here. My prayer has been answered, but now I *preach in chains*! How differently God sometimes answers our prayers!

"I had hope that the church in Rome would sponsor my mission tour to Spain. However, I now realize that will never be possible for me.

"At the conclusion of my third missionary journey in Ephesus, I went about the churches of Asia gathering a collection for poor believers in Jerusalem. This was a wonderful symbol of the unity of the body of Christ. We are one church, Jew and Gentile. For the Gentiles to give so generously to help the Jewish believers in the Holy City was a meaningful gesture.

"On my arrival in Jerusalem, I got in touch immediately with James, the pastor, delivering the gift to him personally. While there I was seen by a group of Jews from Asia in the company of some Gentile believers. Later, I went up to the Temple at the hour of prayer. Going beyond the stones of warning at the Court of Gentiles, I was suddenly surrounded by a mob. They screamed, 'This man has defiled the Temple of God by bringing Gentiles into it!' That was not the case, for my Gentile friends had remained in the outer court. However, a riot ensued. Roman soldiers at the fortress Antonio heard the clamor and came hurriedly down the outer stair into the Temple courtyard. They took me into protective custody. I was to stand trial in Jerusalem on this charge.

"I do believe I could have successfully refuted it. However, my nephew's word came to us in the night that there was a plot on my life. When this information reached the ears of the Roman commander, he had me transferred to Caesarea on the Mediterranean. I spent some time in that Roman city under semiconfinement. I had the run of the government complex but was not allowed to leave Caesarea. During those days, I had opportunity to bear a Christian witness to Governor Felix and later to King Agrippa and Festus. As the time approached for my trial in Jerusalem, I was afraid that I could not get justice there. Being a Roman citizen, I appealed to Caesar. My appeal was correct. However, the rulers' timing in sending me to Rome was poorly chosen. We set out by ship in autumn. I'd sailed the Mediterranean enough to know how dangerous this can be. Sure enough, we were shipwrecked and had to winter in Malta. In the spring, we sailed on to Rome.

"Timothy, I've tried to be all things to all men in order that I might win some to faith in Christ. I am, of course, a Jew, the son of devout parents, members of the tribe of Benjamin. I was privileged to study with Gamaliel in Jerusalem and became a zealous Pharisee. No man has ever had more pride of race and religion than I.

"I am by culture a Greek. As you know, I speak the language fluently. I read the Scriptures in the Septuagint or Greek translation. I have always been proud of my cultural background and opportunities.

"I am also a Roman by citizenship. My father was a magistrate in Tarsus. He established law and order by putting down a threatened insurrection. Rome was so pleased at this that the emperor himself bestowed upon my father Roman citizenship. I've always had a patriotic pride. My citizenship has come in handy, giving me entrée many times with the authorities. Indeed, it brought me to Rome.

"My son, despite all this, I count my Jewish race and religion, my Greek culture, and my Roman citizenship as nothing compared to the knowledge of Christ. He is the most important thing in my life— my conversion, the most significant event in my experience. You know, of course, of my conversion, for I have told you about it many times. It convinced me that Christ is alive and with us. It convinced me that God had called me to be his apostle and that my mission should be to the Gentiles, the new Israel.

"There is so much we have to talk of. I am anxious to learn about your mother, Eunice. I was so sorry to learn in your last letter about the death of your noble grandmother, Lois. Surely, she is present with our Lord. You have had a fortunate spiritual heritage.

"Before I let you go tonight, there is one other

thing that I have been anxious to mention to you. There's a false report abroad about my preaching in Athens. It has come to my attention from some of the believers who visited here a couple of months back. The story is that my preaching on Mars Hill was a failure. That's not so! These people have even taken a line from one of my letters in which I said, 'I have determined to know nothing among you save Christ and him crucified.' They have applied this out of context to mean that my intellectual preaching in Athens was a failure.

"I hope you will remind them when you hear this rumor that it was anything but a failure. Dionysius, a member of the Athens supreme court, was converted that day, along with others. It is true that I did not remain to establish a church in Athens. I became ill, as you will recall, and went on to Corinth where I spent eighteen months in the home of Aquila and Priscilla. However, I have kept in close touch with the believers in Athens, and a flourishing congregation has been established there. Wherever you come across this rumor, please squelch it!

"Timothy, I have so much to say to you, but time will not permit tonight. It's strange, you know. I thought that the older a man got, the less sleep he required. I seem to be the exception to that rule. I want to give you some instructions tomorrow, and I want to hear about your work. Come soon, but not too early.

"Timothy, as you leave, walk through the forum past the Arch of Hadrian. Turn left into short street to the east of the Appian Way. On the left, you will find the shop of a blacksmith. Ask for Rufus. As you inquire about the cost of having a horse shod, make the sign of the fish, *ichthus*, with your rod in the dirt floor of his shop. Rufus will recognize you as a believer. Tell him I sent you, and his hospitality will be yours. You see, Rufus is a deacon of the church here in Rome.

"Timothy, my son, you must make your life a life of study; and you must give attention to the training of the believers in sound doctrine, in ethical living, and in witnessing as they share their faith.

"Thank you for coming. I know you are weary from your journey. I, too, am tired. I will pull this beloved old cloak about my shoulders and lie down in the joy of knowing you are here with me in Rome. Good night, my son. God rest you."

10

Jacob, Man in Miniature
Genesis 32:24-30

"Come my son Benjamin, son of my old age, son of my beloved Rachel. Sit with me by the campfire. Here, wrap my cloak about your shoulders. It's cold tonight. Look at the stars, my son. They are an eternal reminder of God's promise to me and to your grandfather Isaac and to your great-grandfather Abraham. One day God will make of our descendants a great nation.

"The days are passing rapidly for me, like the sparks flying up from that fire—they glow for a moment and soon are no more. Soon I shall be gathered to my fathers. I want you to bury me at Machpelah with Abraham and Sarah, Isaac and Rebekah. Your dear mother is buried north of Bethlehem. I erected a stone pillar above her grave.

"Benjamin, as the youngest of my twelve sons you are my joy. I hope to live on through you. My other son by Rachel, Joseph, is dead—killed by some beast as far as we know. All I have of him is his tattered coat of many hues.

"It was in giving you birth that my Rachel died. With her last breath she named you Ben-oni, son of my ill luck. But the name also means son of my right hand. You look so much like your mother; sometimes I can hardly bear it.

"There are things about your father you should know—things both bad and good. I want you to hear them from me. Here at this camp fire shall be your school. You will hear bits and pieces of your father's past from your brothers, the servants and the women. I don't want you to grow up with a distorted account. You must hear it straight from me.

"Now, Son, I want you to understand that I'm not proud of all my youth. I blush to tell you that my name has not always been Israel. It once was Jacob, which means trickster, supplanter. I was a twin to your uncle Esau. He was born first. They say he was all red and hairy. I was born holding onto his heel. In a sense I've never let it go!

"Your uncle Esau was an outdoorsman; a hunter like the great pharaoh of Egypt. As a boy I stayed close to the tents. I was my mother's boy. Son, my youth was a catalogue of shrewdness and tricks. I traded Esau out of his inheritance with a crock of stew. Much has been lost in a moment's weakness!

"Next I tricked my blind father, Isaac. Being my mother's favorite, she helped me. I made some broth and put goat skin on my arms and neck. Isaac said, 'It is the skin of Esau, but the voice of Jacob.' Anyway, he gave me his blessing which meant I would be entitled to the eldest son's inheritance.

"When Esau found out what I'd done, he was furious. Our mother Rebecca sent me away, promising to send for me once matters had settled down. She never lived to see me return home.

"In exile, I lived with my uncle Laban. I fell in love with Laban's beautiful daughter Rachel. She was a shapely shepherdess. She became the desire of my life. I asked Laban's permission to marry Rachel. For the bride price I was required to work for Laban for seven years. I was so much in love that the years seemed only a few days.

"At the climax of the wedding feast I lifted my bride's veil. Beneath it was Leah, Rachel's dull-eyed and plain sister. I was outraged at Laban. He explained that by custom the oldest girl in a family must be married first. However, Laban said that I might have Rachel as my wife also—for seven more years' work.

"In due course I got even with Laban for his shrewd bargain. The spotted goats and black lambs in the herd and flock were to be mine. I carefully bred the goats and sheep so that most of the offspring were mine. When Laban found out about this, I took Rachel, Leah, and the flocks and fled for home. Rachel also managed to make off with the household clay gods (which entitled me to inherit Laban's wealth at his death).

"Laban came after us and caught up with us. He said he wanted to at least say good-bye to his daughters. (He wanted to find the household gods.) Rachel sat on the clay gods and protested, 'I cannot rise. I am suffering the common lot of women.' We were soon on our way back to Canaan.

"I had been with Laban for twenty years and had accumulated great wealth, flocks and herds. At our parting Laban said, 'The Lord watch between you and me while we are absent one from another.' What that prayer meant was 'May God keep an eye on you and me while we can't keep an eye on each other.'

"Benjamin, I had cheated my brother, my father, and my uncle who was also my father-in-law. The heart is deceitful above all things, and desperately wicked. The heart is a Jacob—you do not know what you are capable of doing until the test comes.

"At long last I was going home—a different man than I went away. I was returning a successful man, with flocks, herds, wives and eleven sons.

"Then I got word Esau was coming to meet me with four hundred armed men! I immediately divided my herd into two portions. Perhaps at least half of them would escape harm. Then I sent a bribe to Esau. I sent nine separate droves of animals, each led by a servant. The servants were instructed to say to Esau, 'These are a present for you. Your servant Jacob is coming.' In this way I hoped to wear down Esau's hostility.

"I spent the night beside the brook Jabbok. I tried to sleep with little success. All night I wrestled with my guilty conscience and fear of what I might face at dawn. My son, your sins will find you out in time and in your conscience. I wrestled with the Lord God that night. By morning he had given me a new name: 'Israel,' which means a prince of God.

"Since that eventful homecoming, I have suffered much. I found that my mother had died. Since then my father Isaac and your brother Joseph have died, as well as your precious mother Rachel, whom we lost on the way home.

"Benjamin, your heart, too, can be a Jacob, a trickster. I pray you my son, let God make you different.

"Enough. It is late. Good night, my son. Shalom."

11
Moses, Supreme Lawgiver
Exodus 3:1-8; 33:1-2,11

The year is 1250 BC. The Hebrews are camped east of the Jordan. Their forty-year wilderness trek is near its end. They are poised now, ready to enter the Land of Promise.

Half way up Mount Nebo a campfire burns. As we draw near, we see two men sitting near the fire. One appears to be an old man with a long white beard. Yet, we will discover that his eyes and his mind are quite keen. The other man looks to be middle-aged. The older man is speaking.

"Eleazar, you've been a faithful scribe to me across these years. I appreciate your making the climb with me and being my companion about the camp fire tonight. I'm in the mood to reminisce. That's what an old man is good at—telling the stories of the past. You've heard most of what I have to say, but I'm anxious that you set the story down accurately for the sons of Israel yet unborn.

"When I was your age, Eleazar, I was a prince in the royal court of Egypt. But that was long ago and far away.

"You've heard the story of my birth to slave

parents. Those were hard days for our people in Egypt. Rameses was the pharaoh who did not remember Joseph and enslaved his descendants. Our people multiplied so that Rameses feared a slave revolt. He decreed that for a time every newborn male should be drowned in the Nile.

"After my birth, my mother, Jochebed, hid me for three months. Hiding a baby is no easy task. Finally, it became impossible to keep my presence secret in our crowded living quarters. My mother told me that she made a watertight basket and placed me in it. Then she set me afloat among the reeds that grew along the bank of the Nile. Miriam, my older sister, was posted to keep watch over the place where I was hidden.

"You should hear Miriam describe the fear she felt as she saw a party of Egyptian women approaching my hiding place. Miriam prayed that I'd be quiet and remain undiscovered. But you can't count on a baby keeping quiet. I let out a scream, Miriam said, and the Egyptian women found me. It turned out that the entourage was that of Pharaoh's daughter. She had no children. She had prayed to Ra, the sun god, that she might have a son. When she found me in the reeds, she felt her prayers had been answered.

"Miriam offered to get a wet nurse for the baby. Thus, my own mother was my nurse in the royal palace. My mother was also my teacher during those early years. I love both my mothers—real and foster.

"As I grew up, Eleazar, I often dreamed that I would come to a position of influence in the government of Egypt; then I might be instrumental in delivering my people from slavery. The Egyptians called our people 'the Habiru' and thus, we have come to call ourselves Hebrews.

"When I was about forty years of age, I tried to help our people by taking a slave's part in a dispute. I was overzealous, for I killed the Egyptian slave master. I thought no one knew about this except the Hebrew I had helped. However, I was soon to learn that the slaves did not appreciate what I'd done on their behalf. Gratitude is a rare quality. The result was that I had to leave the royal palace and flee Egypt.

"I spent the next forty years in exile in Midian. The desert hardly compares favorably with the fertile Nile Valley. I had been a prince in Egypt—grandson of the pharaoh. In Midian I found myself a shepherd. Those years did have their bright spots. I married Zipporah, daughter of Jethro the priest of Midian. Though we were happy, I brooded long hours over the plight of my people in Egypt. If only the God of Abraham would see their plight, hear their prayers, and deliver them.

"Eleazar, it was in the desert of Midian that I met the Lord God. I had learned about him at my mother's knee. I knew all the stories of Abraham, Isaac, Jacob, and Joseph. I knew how God had been real in the lives of those patriarchs. I knew God's promise through them to my people. However, the call of God came to me personally in the desert of Midian.

"I was an old man of eighty when I met Yahweh at the burning bush. (You know the story.) There the Lord said, 'When you have brought forth the people out of Egypt, you shall serve God upon this mountain.' (It was near Mount Horeb or Sinai that I had this call experience.)

"I protested that I was not an eloquent speaker who could persuade Pharaoh to let my people go. Believe me, Eleazar, I did not volunteer to be their deliverer; I was drafted.

"It was strange. One morning I went out as a shepherd tending his flock. The next morning I set out to become shepherd of a nation yet to be formed. How strangely the Lord works in our lives. I've never escaped the compulsion of that clear call from God.

"Across the years I've trusted God's providence and have never had it fail. With God's call came the promise that he would go with me. There were many times of testing. Pharaoh Rameses was an arrogant fellow. He had to be shown that Yahweh is truly God.

"Pharaoh tried repeatedly to strike a compromise with me. At first he said, 'Let your people sacrifice to their god in Egypt. There is no need for them to go into the desert to sacrifice.' This would not do. A plague came. Eleazar, each of the plagues struck down confidence in one of Egypt's gods. Next, Pharaoh relented somewhat, agreeing that we could go, only we were to leave our wives and children in Egypt. That way he was assured of our return. That compromise was equally unacceptable. Finally, Pharaoh agreed to let us go if only we would leave our herds in Egypt. Still, I could not agree. The ultimate plague came on Egypt—the death of their firstborn.

"Eleazar, I had as hard a task rallying the Hebrews as I did contending with the stubborn

Pharaoh. The children of Israel were a rebellious and ungrateful lot. However, they had ample opportunity to behold the providence of God.

"At the Red Sea (or Sea of Reeds as the Egyptians called it), we were in an impossible position. I commanded my people to 'Fear not, stand firm, and see the salvation of the Lord.' He did intervene and deliver us by providing safe passage across the sea and then the destruction of our enemies. In the wilderness, we saw God's providential care repeatedly. He furnished water in the midst of the desert's dryness. He provided manna and quail. He delivered us from our enemies at the oasis of Kadesh-barnea. Yahweh's providence was put to many a test, but it never failed once.

"Across these forty years of wilderness wandering I have sought to act on the known will of God. Dear Scribe, it is not enough to believe in the existence of Yahweh or even to trust in this providence. We must also act on his known will. Across these recent years, I've felt myself to be a man with a task, a mission, a destiny. Frankly, I've felt myself virtually immortal until that task is accomplished. Its realization is at hand now. Look down in the valley at the flickering camp fires. There, across the Jordan, is the Land of Promise. Our people will soon go across the Jordan and take possession of it. However, Eleazar, Joshua will be their leader and not Moses. No, don't protest. I've known this for a long time, and I accept it as the will of God for me.

"You know, for a man of the low Egyptian delta, I've spent lots of my life on the mountaintops. None towers higher than Sinai. There I received the call of God and later received the Ten Words or Commandments. On Sinai I saw the glory of God pass by. There I talked with God as a man talks with a friend, face to face.

"Eleazar, please record these events fairly. While I could reach the heights in intercession for my people, I was often impatient with them. As their leader, I often chafed at their stupidity, such as their worshiping the gold calf at the foot of Mount Sinai. I was also constantly plagued with their murmuring ingratitude. When we had manna and quail in the desert, they complained that they had no garlic and leeks for seasoning!

"Tomorrow you must return to the camp. Me? I will climb to the top of Nebo and get a view of the Promised Land. The camp fire is about out. No, don't get any more wood. It's time for us to sleep. Was there any of that stew left? Thank you. Good night, Eleazar, good friend."

As brilliant and beautiful as the life of Moses was, it too "came short of the glory of God." Every human attainment is "not yet," incomplete, compared with the promises of God.

Moses climbed Mount Nebo. "And the Lord said to Moses, 'This is the land I [promised] to Abraham . . . I have let you see it with your eyes, but you shall not go over there'" (Deut. 34:4, RSV).

Moses died in the land of Moab, but there is one greater than Moses. His name is Jesus of Nazareth, the Christ.

12
David—Shepherd, Warrior, King
2 Samuel 18:28-33

The setting of our story is in the thirtieth year of King David's forty-year reign. He is in a small desert wilderness town, Mahanaim, along with his troops. The townspeople have brought in food for the men; and now, David is talking with three of his generals. They are laying plans for the battle of Ephraim Wood. Absalom, King David's son, whom he loves dearly, is leading a rebellion against his father. Let's listen to at least one side of the conversation, as the king and his generals make their plans.

"Joab, you've been my commanding general for all these years. You know the woods of Ephraim like the back of your hand. Indeed, there is not very much of this entire land you and I haven't fought over together in years past. Now, here's the plan. Joab, I want you to guard the pass that allows entrance into the wood. And then, Abishai, you are to take the wadi to the south. Secret your men in there. Keep their presence quiet and wait for the trumpet signal from Joab. Then, Ittai, you are to take your men to the north ridge. You will have them surrounded. And when those raw enemy troops march into that wood, they'll not be suspecting a thing! We'll take them by complete surprise! I tell you, they'll be no match for my seasoned veterans. Indeed, I will lead the battle myself! What? What do you mean, I shouldn't do it, I'm too valuable? Oh, my word! But I've always . . . all right, you're persuasive. I'll remain here. Joab, you're in command. Now, be off with you. You must take your positions before the enemy arrives. Remember, for my sake, don't harm the young prince Absalom!

"Who's that? Oh, well, yes, of course, Shobi. No I don't want my crown. Heavy is the head that wears the crown. I simply want this matter soon over and well concluded. Come, come and sit with me. I must wait for the news of the battle. It seems that a king spends most of his life waiting for something or someone. That's hard for a man of action. What? Oh, all right.

(The king calls to the watchtower.) "Watchman, this is King David, I'll stay here between the outer and inner city gates. Let me know the moment you see a runner on the horizon. Very well.

"You know, Shobi, I grew up not far from here, down in Bethlehem. I was a shepherd when I was a lad, looking after my father, Jesse's, sheep. Indeed, those days seem long ago and far away. I remember them fondly. It's interesting, when you look back on your youth, how bright and calm and smooth everything seems to have been. I had nothing more serious to do than to look after my father's sheep, to find them water and grass, and to see that they were secure during the night hours. Those were simple days. These are cruel and crude days, when human flesh is cheap, even the flesh of kings, mind you. Well, things seemed so placid then.

"I know this much, I had a simple faith in God as a youth, a very simple faith. I placed my trust in him. 'The Lord is my light and my salvation; whom shall I fear? The Lord is the strength of my life; of whom shall I be afraid?' Mmmm . . . I had a deep longing to know and to love the Almighty. 'As the hart panteth after the water brooks, so panteth my soul after thee.' 'The Lord, he is my shepherd, I shall not want.' Maybe those days were not as simple as I recall. I remember, for example, an encounter with a bear and another with a lion. Of course, those stories have grown with the telling across the years, you understand!

"There was one time in my youth when I became very dissatisfied with my lot as a shepherd. You see, my three older brothers were in King Saul's army. Yes, indeed. And I was envious of them, for they were at the front. They were where things were happening, where Saul and his troops were facing the Philistines. Our King Saul fought the Philistines all his life, all his reign.

"Mmmm . . . I remember how excited I was one day when my father called me and gave me some parched grain, some loaves of bread, and some cheeses, and sent me to the front to check on my brothers. Oh, I made that journey in a hurry you may be sure. When I got to the front, that Goliath affair was afoot. You know that story. Every child knows that story. I was young, and I had a clear faith in God.

Maybe I was a little foolhardy, as well. God gave me the victory.

"I had no idea that such an event would propel me into instant popularity. I received King Saul's reward and his soldiers' praise. When we got back to the capital in Hebron, that's when the trouble began. As we went into the city, it seemed that every girl and woman had gathered from the countryside for miles around. They were singing. It was a lovely sight and a lovely sound. They were singing about King Saul. How the king loved that! They sang, 'Saul, has slain his thousands!' Then they sang, 'But David, his tens of thousands.' Little did I imagine that my popularity would get me into trouble with the king. Saul became insanely jealous. For a time I had the favor of the court and played for him when he was in his deep and dark moods. Still he was terribly jealous. Twice I almost lost my life to his javelin. That was a torturous time.

"The king called me in one day. I stood before him, and he said, 'Any man with your bravery and raw courage deserves the king's reward.'

"I said, 'But sire, I have received your reward and a generous one at that.'

"'No, no,' said he, 'You shall have the king's daughter for your wife.'

"'How could one of such lowly birth as I aspire to be the son-in-law of the king of Israel?' I asked. He promised me his oldest daughter, Merab, but then changed his mind and gave her to someone else. He had another daughter, Michal. She had been in that crowd that day when the women sang. One of the king's captains told me she was very much in love with the young hero!

"Much to my amazement the king promised to give me Michal to be my bride. There was a condition however. I was to go out with a band of men and succeed in killing a hundred Philistines and bring proof of my deed to King Saul. Well, love is enough to motivate a man to do anything! I can assure you I went out with great zeal.

"We fell upon a group of Philistines, and I brought back proof to Saul of the death of two hundred. I counted out the proof in his presence. He had to keep his word, and he gave me Michal for my bride. During the night, Saul told his son, Jonathan, my closest friend, of his intention to see me done to death. Jonathan came to the bedchamber and gave me word, and on my wedding night, I slipped out into the darkness and ran from the wrath of the king. Saul was determined to have me dead, and he pursued me. I became a fugitive in the land.

"There are many things related to that I'd like to tell you—about the shewbread and the killing of the priests. But let me say that on one occasion I came upon Saul in a cave. I could have easily taken his life, but I had too much respect for the Lord's anointed. I cut off the hem of his garment and thereby demonstrated that I'd been near enough to cut out his heart but had spared him. This seemed to calm his anger for a time, but it soon returned. I was left to wander among the Philistines, my enemies. I had to pretend insanity. I drooled on my beard and walled my eyes and looked so wild that the Philistines were quite sure I was crazy. Thus, I passed the years separated from my beloved Michal, whom the king gave to another man as wife. And I was separated from my friend, Jonathan.

"After a time King Saul went to fight the Philistines in the region of Gilboa. He and his men were so pressed by the enemy that his armor was pierced by their arrows, wounding him seriously. He turned to his armor bearer and asked him to take his sword and kill him. The man was afraid to kill the king, so Saul fell on his own sword and took his own life. The armor bearer, seeing what had happened, did the same thing to himself. Not only did King Saul die that day but also his sons died with him, and among them, my friend, Jonathan.

"It was a dark, dark day in the history in Israel. I recall the lament I offered: 'How are the mighty fallen! Tell it not in Gath, publish it not in the streets of Askelon!' It was a dark day that made me king of Israel. I was crowned in Hebron and made it my capital for seven years. You know, of course, I have since captured the city of Jerusalem, the Jebusite city. It was the Jebusite city of Salem, the city of peace. I've made it both my political and my religious capital.

"Ah, I've known good days, long years of exciting warfare, and victory after victory. In the spring of the year, I would take my raiding party and we would make our way down into the plain of Sharon. We would fall upon the unsuspecting Philistines and carry off their treasure and women. We would always come back to our mountain fortress in Jerusalem. (I had to leave Jerusalem the other day on foot.)

"There were good days, but there were evil days too. You know that story, I'm sure. One spring I was not allowed to go into battle, even as I was not allowed to go into battle today, for fear that I might meet a fate like King Saul's. I tried to pass the time. In my mind were the sounds and sights and smells of war. I could see the sun reflecting off the brass shields of my troops and the enemies'. I could see the arrows and javelins flying through the air. I could hear the neighing of the war horses, the clash of metal swords on shields and armor, the cries of the wounded and dying.

"That night I saw Bathsheba and fell in love with her. Though she was married to Uriah, I took her. Later, I had Joab place Uriah in the heat of the battle, then fall back, leaving him to die at the hands of the enemies.

"I became miserable after that experience. The song went out of my heart, and I no longer cared to play the harp. I no longer cared to compose songs. It was a dark, dark time. I shall always be grateful to the Almighty for sending his prophet Nathan with that silly story about a man who had a great flock of sheep and another poor man who had one little lamb. The rich man took the poor man's lamb and slaughtered it to feed his friends. I became enraged at such a thing and said, 'That man deserves to die!' Then Nathan pointed his long, bony finger underneath my royal nose and said, 'Thou art the man!' Oh, how can I ever forget that? It's strange how ugly our sins appear in the lives of others. I repented, and God forgave me.

"There have been hard, heartbreaking days since then. My son by Bathsheba lived only a week and died. Later, Absalom, on whom I set my hopes, broke my heart. Oh, what a dandy is Absalom! That long hair, clear to his waist. He cuts some figure as a soldier. He rides a white mule. You don't have to try to find him in a crowd. He's a fancy dresser. He always wears the brightest colors. He has no son of his own. Wanting to be remembered he has erected a monument to himself in the King's Valley or the Kidron Valley. He expects to be buried there.

"Watchman, anyone on the horizon? Very well. Let me know.

"Oh, my son, Absalom. The heartbreak he's brought me! He murdered his brother, Amnon, for the rape of their sister, Tamar. Then he stole away the hearts of the men of Israel. He seduced the loyalty of my followers. He came into Jerusalem, riding that white mule. When the great lines of men stood outside the judgment hall waiting to be heard; or when one came away not liking my judgment, Absalom would take him aside and put an arm about his shoulder and say, 'Oh, that I were king in Israel.' He said that often enough they got the idea! He's now leading this rebellion, Shobi. He has raised an army, a motley army of raw recruits. They will be no match for Joab and my seasoned veterans; those shopkeepers, herdsmen, and husbandmen. We'll cut them to ribbons.

"Watchman, what? Someone's coming? Very good, a runner! Send him, send him in the gate. I'll await his message here.

"Ah, there lad, get your breath. What word of the battle? Victory, you say? We slaughtered them, you say? Twenty thousand men dead in the course of a single day! But tell me, young prince Absalom— what of Absalom, my son? No word? You don't know. You saw a commotion in the woods, but you are not sure about its outcome? Stand aside, stand over there.

"Ah, another runner! Send him this way. Yes, yes! Tell me, man, I've heard of the victory, but what of my son, Absalom, the young prince? I gave instruction that no harm was to come to him.

"What? You would to God that all the king's enemies were as Absalom? Caught by his hair in the limbs of an oak tree? The mule went from under him? Three spears? Buried in a pit in the woods of Ephraim covered with stones?

"Oh, my son, my son, Absalom! Oh, would to God that I had died for thee! My son, my son, Absalom, Absalom, Absalom, my son, my son!"

13

Hosea: A Broken Home Provides a Gospel
Hosea 1:2-3; 3:1-3

"My name is Hosea and I am a prophet of the Lord God, Yahweh. My preaching ministry over-lapped that of Amos in Israel, the Northern King-dom. Amos means 'burden' for he carried the weight of the sins of his people. I was influenced by Amos, and my message, certainly my early prophesying, contained a strong note of judgment. I preached against sin and warned of the peril at hand unless the people repented and returned to the Lord.

"For nearly half a century our country enjoyed a political golden age. It was an era of peace. King Uzziah was king in Judah in the south, and Jeroboam II ruled in Israel. The two of them were in power for almost forty years. This gave our countries a time of political stability. Another factor which certainly con-tributed to peace was the fact that no great power was dominating the politics of our region. Egypt was dreaming of glories past; and Assyria, a sleeping giant, was not yet aware of its might.

"The time also saw great economic prosperity in Israel and Judah. Caravan trade brought riches into our area. However, the rich grew richer and oppressed the poor. Amos lashed out against the social injustices of our time.

"Recent days have brought violent changes. King Jeroboam died, and we've had many kinglets in rapid succession. Some died at the hands of assassins. Furthermore, the new Assyrian king, Tiglath-pileser, is threatening our borders. The cities are filled with awesome rumors of invasion and war. These are tense times.

"The Word of the Lord came to me while I was a young man. Before I was married, I was God's prophet.

"One day, in a neighboring village, I met Gomer. She was the loveliest girl in all the land. She had a soft olive complexion, dancing dark eyes, and a smile that could melt a man at a hundred paces. I courted her, and wonder of wonders, I won Gomer to be my wife. I was the happiest man alive! It was too good to be true, and yet it was. The whole village turned out for our wedding, and we received the congratulations and best wishes of all.

"I took Gomer to my stone cottage as my bride. I loved her with all my heart—with a love that was deeper and more lasting than I could realize at that time. You see, I had no idea how bittersweet love could be.

"Within a year our first child was born—a son! I named him Jezreel which means, 'God sows.' Surely, he was the fruit of our love and the gift of God. Life was complete, and all joy. Long hours in the barley fields, from sunup till sunset, were no burden for I could go home to Gomer and little Jezreel.

"One evening at dusk I was returning from the barley field and I saw a dim figure dash from the cottage into a grove of trees. There she was joined by a man. They hurried down the path to the road which leads into town. I found little Jezreel unattended and crying. There was a note. I staggered as though I'd been hit! A woman can be a man's heaven—or his hell.

"In the village, Gomer was laughing with her lovers, not at a tavern but at a temple. She had become a voluntary temple prostitute in the worship of Baal. A so-called 'holy woman,' she had dedicated herself to the fertility worship during their pagan spring festival.

"When she came home, after the week of festival was concluded, there were no apologies, no words of regret. There was only that silly little smile. I seethed inside and finally exploded, but it made no difference. Gomer was apparently lacking a conscience. The thing that's hard to believe is that I loved her still—despite her unfaithfulness.

"In time Gomer gave birth to a daughter. Now in Hebrew the prefix 'lo' means 'not.' I named the child 'Lo-ruhamah' which means 'no more mercy.'

"When the winter rains were over, the time for the pagan festival came again. Gomer left again, as before. She later had a third child, a boy. I named him 'Lo-ammi' which means 'not mine'!

"I have no words to adequately describe the agony and anguish of those days. Gomer had been pure, lovely, and attractive when I married her. Now she was playing the fool before all the world. I tell you, it was demonic, more than a man can stand.

"The next spring Gomer left and did not return. She left me and the children to become a cultic prostitute, a permanent member of the Baal temple staff. She said her lovers provided her with rich foods (raisin cakes), wine, and gifts, while I gave her nothing.

"I had to stop preaching for two reasons. Who would listen to a prophet whose wife had become a harlot? And what message had I to give? It was a dark and difficult period in my life. I brooded, wept, and asked God 'Why?' How could even God bring anything good out of this stark tragedy? He had called me to prophesy, and he had given me lovely Gomer as my wife. Now there was only loneliness, shame, and a broken heart. I still loved her—which added to my agony.

"Can you believe it, in Gomer's unfaithfulness and my continuing love for her, I found a gospel? In my deep grief, there was a saving word from God. You see, I got a glimpse of God's love for Israel in what I'd suffered: God had loved and wooed Israel, like a lovely maiden in Egypt. He had brought her out of slavery by his might and provided for her tenderly through the wilderness experience. Then he brought her safely into Canaan, the land of milk and honey—and she loved Baal instead of the Lord! She worshiped the pagan god of fertility to ensure the fertility of her crops and herds, instead of the Lord of all creation. But God loves Israel still, despite her sin, even as I love Gomer. God said to me, 'How can I give you up, O Ephraim! How can I hand you over, O Israel!' (Hos. 11:8, RSV). God's heart was broken by Israel's idolatry, as my heart was broken by Gomer's harlotry! Yet God loves us, despite our sin. My message became one of grace and not simply judgment. For you see, I loved Gomer, my adultrous wife 'even as the Lord loves his people, Israel.'

"The years passed—years of loneliness and shame, grief and heartbreak. Then one day I learned that the temple of Baal had finished with Gomer. With the passing of time, her beauty had faded. She was no longer called for by the male worshipers. She had been grossly used and abused by those lustful men; some of them the very men who had congratulated me on our wedding day. The initial thrill and excitement for Gomer had passed long before. Only the filth and self-loathing were left. A thousand nights had turned into a dull numbness or a shrieking nightmare. Sin had promised Gomer much, but it delivered something vastly different from what she had expected. Now the temple of Baal and her lovers were throwing her out, literally. She was being sold as a slave!

"While I was musing on this turn of events, the word of the Lord came to me. 'Hosea,' he said, 'go and buy Gomer back.'

"'Lord, you can't be serious.' I replied.

"'I am serious. You still love her, don't you?'

"'Yes,' I said.

"'Then go and buy her back,' God said.

"I left the children with a neighbor and made my

way down the road to town; down the same road
Gomer had traveled with her lovers. A crowd was
gathered at the city gate for the auction.

"What a sight! Gomer had aged far beyond her
years. She had become haggard and hardened. Her
hair was disheveled and the light had gone out in her
eyes. She was a pitiful sight!

"I asked the auctioneer what price she was to
bring. With a sneer, he said, 'Thirty pieces of silver,
the price of a common slave!'

"But I only have fifteen. How much barley
would you take for the balance?'

'A homer and a half,' said he.

"Eight bushels, almost my whole crop. Fifteen
pieces of silver and a homer and a half of barley.
That's almost a year's wages! Still I could hear the
words, 'Hosea, go and buy back Gomer.' I hurried
home and returned with the load of barley. The deal
was closed.

"By this time everyone in the village was asking,
'Why would you buy Gomer back?'

"'Because I love her, even as the Lord God,
Yahweh, loves this sinning nation,' I replied. My
preaching suddenly had an authentic ring about it,
due to what I'd endured.

"I brought Gomer home again, for the first time
in a long time. I spoke to her tenderly, yet firmly:
'You must dwell in my house for many days. You shall
not play the harlot again, nor belong to another man.'

"With the passing of time our attitudes softened
and love grew. To be sure, it was never again as it had
once been, but there was great improvement in our

relationship. I changed the name of Lo-ruhamah to Ruhamah, 'Beloved,' and Lo-ammi to Ammi, 'My own.'

"Now I can preach grace and God's suffering love. I learned much through heartbreak. I learned something of how God feels toward his erring children. He, too, is heartbroken by our sin, but loves us still. I also learned that all sin is really against covenant love, and that the root of sin is deserting God for something or someone else.

"I loved Gomer in spite of all she did wrong. *How much more* does God love us?

"My message is simple, 'Repent, return, come home to the God who loves you enough to make you and then buy you back.'"

14
Haman's Harvest of Hatred
Esther 7—10

The time is the mid fifth century BC. The scene is Susa, one of the three principal capitals of the Persian Empire. Persia stretched from the Aegean Sea to India with its 127 provinces governed by satraps. It included areas of Babylon, the former kingdom of the Medes, Egypt, Asia Minor, and parts of Greece. The supreme ruler was Ahasuerus, or Xerxes, whose titles included "King of Kings" and "King of Lands" for he was ruler of the entire civilized world.

Our principal character is Haman, the prime minister, who is second only to the king in position and power. Haman was not a Persian, but an Amalekite, just as Napoleon was not a Frenchman, but an Italian Corsican; Hitler was not a German, but an Austrian; and Stalin was not a Russian, but a Georgian. Let us hear Haman:

"My name is Haman. My friends call me 'The Magnificent,' a title not to be disparaged. Obviously, I am only a little short of a genius as an administrator, or I could not have risen to such dizzying heights. You see I am the chief of princes, the president of satraps, second only to Xerxes (by the grace of the god Marduk), king of all the civilized world!

"About a year ago we had a seven-day banquet. It was the grandest affair of state within my memory. The satraps from all the 127 provinces, their chief wives, and aides were in attendance. They came from the points of the compass to the summer capital here at Susa. They were fascinatingly different in their dress and customs, but all shared common allegiance and loyalty to Xerxes. Believe me, it was a show of wealth and splendor, the like of which the world has never seen. It seemed there were tons of gold and silver brought along with the most magnificent and ingenuous gifts to honor our lord, Xerxes. The food, wine, and dancing girls were the finest the kingdom could boast. We even drank from golden goblets.

"The banquet hall had been recently built by our great king. Its mosaic floor of marble, mother of pearl, and precious stones is surely the most beautiful thing of its kind in all the world. Magnificent drapes hung from silver rods and rings.

"Queen Vashti, a woman of matchless beauty, held a banquet for the women as well. At the height of the banquets on the seventh day, the king sent seven eunuchs to bring her to the banquet hall so that he might boast of her beauty before his leaders. To the amazement of us all, she refused to come. The king became absolutely enraged at such audacity! Queen Vashti was setting a bad example of disobedience for all the women of the realm. This word would fly like wildfire. It could well encourage all wives to revolt against their husbands. The king acted rightly, on my personal advice, of course, when he banished her from the realm.

"Once the great banquet of state was concluded, the next major order of business was the selection of a new queen. A royal decree went out, and beautiful virgins were brought in from the entire empire. They were given the best of food and the finest cosmetics, along with a twelve-month training course in beauty and poise.

"Among these virgins was Esther. Her name means 'Star' in our language. In her native tongue, which was Hebrew, her name was Hadassah. She had been reared by her cousin, Mordecai, whose family had come from Jerusalem following its conquest by Nebuchadnezzar. Esther was careful to keep her nationality a secret. She was, on the appointed day, brought into the presence of his royal majesty, the king, by seven handmaidens. She had such beauty, such grace, and charm, the king was left absolutely speechless. He was obviously struck by her startling loveliness. It was plain to see that the king immediately preferred Esther. He gave the command, and the royal crown was brought and placed on her head. She was declared to be the queen of all the civilized world.

"The king declared it a festive occasion. A great banquet was prepared; gifts were passed out to the poor, and taxes were remitted for a season. During the time of this second banquet, two would-be assassins were discovered. Indeed, they were reported to Queen Esther by Mordecai, her cousin and foster father. The queen told Xerxes of this dastardly plot. An investigation was held, and the assassins were hanged. The incident was recorded in the royal chronicles.

"I was second in the kingdom and obviously had the king's ear and confidence. If I may say so modestly, I ran the kingdom, fixing the royal signet practically at will. Great honor was paid me.

"One experience is etched indelibly in my memory. One day I came with royal dignity down the palace steps. Gathered in the courtyard was a great throng of men. Their white robes looked like the snow on the crest of Mount Ararat. They all bowed to the ground—every one of them, with the single exception of Mordecai. I was infuriated that he would not bow. It must have simply been because I am an Amalekite and our people have been ancient enemies. His audacity gnawed at my insides. His stubborn face was before me day and night. No matter where I went or what I was about, I could not get his smug, bearded face out of my mind. Never mind the thousands who were bowing; one did not!

"During my bath one morning, an idea came. It was a failure-proof plot to destroy not only Mordecai, but all the Jews in the Persian Empire. That would teach him and my father's ancient enemies! I dressed hurriedly and hastened to the king's chamber. 'Your Majesty,' I said, 'there is a certain people in the midst of our kingdom who live by a different law. They do not keep the king's law. It is not appropriate that we should tolerate them longer. Let a decree be drawn which will declare that on the thirteenth day of the twelfth month this race of people will be destroyed, men, women, and children, and their goods plundered. Obviously, the execution of such an order will be costly; therefore, I propose to pay 10 thousand talents of silver into his majesty's royal treasury to defray the cost of the issuance of the decree!' 'Do as you will,' said the king, giving me his signet ring. Immediately upon going out, I called the royal secretaries and dictated the edict. Copies were sent on their way that very day by courier to every satrap in the kingdom.

"On receiving word of what was afoot, Mordecai dressed in sackcloth and ashes and was found early in the morning wailing at the king's gate. Of course, he could not come into the palace area so dressed; therefore, Mordecai had a copy of the decree sent to the queen. There was fasting, weeping, and mourning, not only on his part but also on the part of all the Jews who were within the city. Among themselves these strange people declared a three-day feast.

"The queen, of course, could not enter the royal court unbidden, on penalty of death. She had not seen the king in thirty days. Therefore, I marveled at her courage when she did enter the royal presence. Xerxes, who loved her deeply, held out his scepter to her. She touched it, and the king suggested that she might make any request her heart could desire. He would grant it up to half the kingdom. Her request, as my aide told me, was simple enough. It was that the king and Haman come to dinner with her the next day. The king dispatched my aide immediately to tell me of the honor. Indeed, how proud I felt to have dinner with the queen in the presence of the king. A royal dinner for the three of us; and, after all, I was, in a sense, royalty.

"We went to dine that lovely midday on the colonnaded terrace outside the queen's chambers. Servants attended our every wish and kept us comfortable with long, plumed fans. The table was set in a delightful fashion, and the food was superb. The queen was such a beauty. Her eyes were like deep pools, her complexion was so fair, her hair immaculate, her shoulders so white and round, any man would feel attracted to her. If only I were king—but enough of that! We ate fruit and other delicacies; and while we were drinking wine, the king asked again what her petition might be. She said simply that 'tomorrow you and Haman would join me on the terrace again for dinner.'

"I went out quite exuberant. I felt not only joy but also a great sense of honor and self-esteem; but as I rounded the corner and started down the stairway, I caught sight of Mordecai—horrid, despicable Mordecai! I became troubled and filled with wrath. I could hardly restrain myself from plunging my silver dagger into his heart. Why wait for the thirteenth day of the twelfth month?

"On reaching home, Zeresh, my wife, tried to comfort me. She recounted my vast riches, my large number of sons, the great and high position I held above all the princes of the realm, and the fact that even Queen Esther had invited me to dine with her and the king.

"But I could never be content as long as Mordecai breathes. Then Zeresh, with her typical insight, suggested, 'Have a gallows built, fifty cubits high. Tell the king in the morning to hang Mordecai on it, then go merrily to dinner.' The plan was set in motion. I went to sleep that night to the sound of hammers in the distance and such sweet sleep—sweet revenge seemed satisfying to my soul!

"Unknown to me, the very hammers that put me to sleep must have been resounding in the royal chamber. Something caused royal insomnia. The king, being unable to sleep, called for the historians to come and read the chronicles. If the reading of history cannot put one to sleep, one is beyond help. During the reading the historian came upon the account of Mordecai's warning. The king asked, 'Has this man been rewarded?' He received a negative answer.

"The king slept late the next morning. When I entered his presence, he asked, 'What shall I do for the man whom the king delights to honor?' Well, indeed, whom would the king delight to honor more than my own worthy self? How grand! With a little thought, I came up with an appropriate suggestion. I said, 'O King, live forever. Let the royal robes be brought (those splendid garments of glory). Let them be put on the man in whom the king delights. Let the king's horse be brought for him whom the king delights to honor and let the crown be set upon his head. Let him be led through the city with a worthy official proclaiming before him, 'Behold, this is the man whom the king delights to honor.'

"His majesty said, 'A splendid suggestion! Do

this. You lead the horse through the city for Mordecai, the Jew.' I fled home. Such agony. Such humiliation! What a fate worse than death. Had all the gods conspired against me? Sweet revenge had been so close at hand that I could savor its taste. O, that I should be so mortified!

"In the evening, the king's eunuch summoned me to dinner. The meal was delightful, but I had no taste for it. The wine was heady, but it did not ease my pain. Xerxes asked the third time for the queen's petition. She said, "Sire, my people are going to be killed.'

"'Who is going to do this?'

"'A foe—an enemy. This wicked Haman.'

"The king's wrath was obvious. He turned without a word and walked into the garden. Sheer terror gripped me. Cold beads of perspiration popped out on my forehead. I pled, I begged Queen Esther! I was on her couch as the king returned, pleading for my very life. 'You plot to destroy my queen. There, that gallows which I see from the garden. Why is it there?'

"'Haman had it built for Mordecai,' said the queen.

"'Hang Haman on it!' ordered Xerxes."

It is morning as workmen enter the city gate with its winged bulls. They suddenly come upon the grim gallows with its swinging victim robed like royalty.

"Who can that be?" asked one.

"Why, it's Haman, hanging on the gallows he had us build for Mordecai!"

Woe to the man who lets one critic, one unresponsive person, one unappreciative man spoil his joy.

Woe to the man who seeks revenge. "Vengeance is mine, I will repay, says the Lord."

15
I Am an Offering Plate
Mark 12:41-44

I am an offering plate. I had my start more than ninety years ago on a mountainside in Oregon. You see, I'm made of myrtle wood. It is mentioned in the Old Testament, and it grows only in the Holy Land and on the Pacific Coast of the United States. My brothers and I have been in the Lord's service here at First Baptist Church for twenty-three years—since the construction of this building.

I faced many dangers in my youth. When I was no more than a sprout I was fearful of being stepped on by a deer or crushed by a falling limb. I survived my sapling stage (as people and trees do) and grew into a leafy tree. I remember how proud I was the day I was tall enough for my topmost leaves to see the sunrise. I felt full grown that day. I grew in maturity and gained girth (as trees and people do).

One day I attracted a lumber crew. Their leader barked some orders and a chain saw was placed at my base. I was notched, felled, trimmed, and then snaked to the mill by a tractor. It was painful, let me tell you! I was sawed and planed; turned, sanded, and shellacked. Little did I know that I was being prepared for a high calling!

One day I was shipped from the factory to my new home. I was one of the last things placed in the sanctuary. I will never forget when I was first unwrapped and placed on the Lord's Supper table! The sanctuary was simply breathtaking with its fourteen columns, arches, and row upon row of pews, all stained my color. And the six massive chandeliers! They were so beautiful. I didn't miss my mountainside at all—except for the sound of the wind in the trees. I was lonely for that until one Sunday morning. The sanctuary was filled, and every smiling face seemed so happy. Suddenly, the organ began to play. It was magnificent music such as I'd never heard before, even more lovely than the winds in the trees in Oregon. I wish you all could have been here that first Sunday and every Sunday since, as I have.

You see, I serve in the worship of God. My brother plates and I collect the people's tithes and offerings. It is a thrilling moment. The choir sings as we work. Then the people stand and praise God in a doxology or gloria. We are brought to the front with military precision by the deacons or junior deacons, and the people's gifts are dedicated to God with a prayer.

I never apologize for my work. It's never a chore but always a joy. You see, I give people an opportunity to be obedient children of God—a chance to be part of something bigger than they are, the kingdom of God! I give them a chance to share the gospel with Greensboro, North Carolina, the nation, and the world. I know it's hard to believe, but my brother plates and I have handled millions of dollars, all in voluntary gifts, all dedicated to the glory of God!

Those Who Give

I get close to people. And you can tell a lot about a person by the look on his face while he's reaching for his wallet!

I must admit that some give grudgingly—as though they were having a front tooth extracted. It's interesting how they suddenly become engrossed in the sunlight coming through the windows, the flower arrangement, the flags, or the music. Quickly, the offering plate appears, and they reach for their purse or wallet—too late. It's like a Carolina fumble! They can't hold up the service, you know, so they let the plate pass.

Or, sometimes, they give a quarter. They palm it and make sure it hits the green felt pad—very quietly. On that rare occasion when they do put a twenty dollar bill in the plate, they crease it and put it in with a grand gesture, as if they expected the organ to burst into "Ruffles and Flourishes!" Nothing is more interesting than people—giving.

We have some members who are tippers, rather than tithers. They give a dollar a week, when they come. Yet these very folks sound off, as "paying members," that the church is not giving enough to missions (fifty cents?). Or they often complain that the church is neglecting the youth or the elderly or some other group. The tippers want to see the church add three new staff members when their total gifts wouldn't pay one staff member's Social Security tax.

However, I'm happy to report that most of our

members are generous givers. They give modestly
through an offering envelope, but they give happily
and well. I can detect a look of satisfaction on the face
of a generous giver. I'm sure he or she has a joy in
being a significant part of this great church, in
sharing, and in being obedient to God. It's always a
joy for me to take their offerings to the Lord.

How We Give

Let me surprise you by saying that no one gives a
lot. Many people think ours is a church filled with
rich people. That just isn't so! Last year we only had
six members who gave more than $4,000. We only
had seventy-one out of 2,800 resident members who
gave as much as $1,250 a year. Three of our staff
ministers are in the top 15 percent of givers, so you
know that no one person or group gives a lot. There
is no member in our church who *could* give our
budget goal or a significant part of it. This budget
requires *all* the people doing their part.

It is true, I'm afraid, that too many of our
members miss the joy of giving. Out of 2,800 members, 905 gave nothing last year, according to the
records (and 662 of these are adult members). The
average church in North Carolina has only 300
members! We have three times that number who
neither pledge nor give. That's sad. Or consider that
592 members give a dollar or less a week (and 357 of
these are adults). Seven percent of our members (192)
gave 42 percent of the church's income last year
($308,824). The average annual gift is $267 or a tithe
on $2,670—when the average Greensboro family

makes $14,404 a year. If all our members tithed their income, the church budget would be two million plus dollars!

It is also true that many of our members do give consistently and generously. We had $737,584 given by 1,850 of our members in the past twelve months. I can remember when our offerings were a third that size! Our people have been consistent givers for sixty-five years, leading the state's churches in missions support.

Consider the Good Our Giving Does

Only God really knows. Much of the value of our giving is unseen. For example, let me tell you about our fellowship offering. It is received on first Sundays, usually following the observance of the Lord's Supper. It is confidentially administered by a small deacon committee. It buys milk for children who have lost their father (and family income). It helps a traveler en route home. It helps a nursing home patient or a family who has been burned out.

Think about the good our church's ministries accomplish. The services are carried to shut-ins and hospital patients by radio. I enjoy seeing our silent members at worship and their interpreter. It's a delight to hear our special class sing. Our senior citizens have many activities. Have you heard about the ADY club? (The letters stand for "Ain't Done Yet.") There are luncheons and tours and congregate feeding and fellowship. I've heard some folks talking about a planned high rise to provide housing for the aging near the church.

There are many recreational ministries: teams of every sort, tennis lessons, ceramics, family recreation, even weight watching.

Think about the beautiful worship services here at First Baptist—the choirs, handbells, solos, sermons, and prayers. It's so beautiful, majestic, and thrilling! It's enough to make your sap flow!

Many religious education opportunities are provided by our church. These include 1,100 persons every Sunday in the year (on the average) involved in Bible study. There are also youth and adult seminars, study groups, the mid-week services, Vacation Bible Schools, with more than 500 youngsters, and a great missionary education program. Youth of the church not only have activities and retreats, but also take part in serious Bible study and missions work. All this is led by a host of dedicated volunteers and staff ministers.

Think about our facilities; they are fantastic and adequate. I heard one custodian tell someone that these buildings are used "eight days a week" by all kinds of groups.

Time will not permit me to begin to tell the good our giving does beyond Greensboro. It helps support seven North Carolina colleges and six Southern Baptist seminaries. It helps provide children's homes and retirement homes. It helps support the *Biblical Recorder*, the state Baptist paper—which has the largest circulation of any newspaper in North Carolina!

Our giving helps support Central Chapel with its rich ministry. Our new Southeast Chapel is an exciting new church in the making. Sixteen families there have raised $10,000 toward a down payment on a new site and first building since May. Our church borrowed $17,500 to complete the down payment.

Across America we help support 2,500 missionaries working in the inner cities, with minorities, and in new churches. Overseas, we help support 2,600 missionaries in eighty-six countries to the tune of $51,000,000 a year from Southern Baptist churches. They conduct schools and seminaries, hospitals and clinics, evangelism and broadcasting, agriculture and the establishing of new churches. Children are fed and taught. Those in need are helped. The sick are healed.

I'm proud to be an offering plate at First Baptist of Greensboro. I'm serving the Lord and blessing lives. Aren't you glad to be a part of this great church and its far-reaching ministry? Do your part!

Bibliography

Brown, David. *Dramatic Narrative Preaching.* Valley Forge: Judson Press, 1981.

Buechner, Frederick. *Telling the Truth: The Gospel as Tragedy, Comedy, and Fairy Tale.* New York: Harper and Row, 1977.

Cox, James W. *A Guide to Biblical Preaching.* Nashville: Abingdon Press, 1976.

Craddock, Frederick. *Overhearing the Gospel.* Nashville: Abingdon Press, 1978.

Davis, H. Grady. *Design for Preaching.* Philadelphia: Fortress Press, 1958. See "A Story Told," p. 157.

Jensen, Richar. *Telling the Story: Variety and Imagination in Preaching.* Minneapolis: Augsburg Press, 1979.

Jones, E. Winston. *Preaching and the Dramatic Arts.* New York: The Macmillan Co., 1948. See "The Art of Using Story-Material."

Macartney, Clarence Edwar. *Preaching Without Notes.* Nashville: Abingdon Press, 1946. See "Bible Biographical Preaching."

McEachern, Alton H. *Proclaim the Gospel.* Nashville: Convention Press, 1975. (See pp. 57 and following for a discussion of "innovations in preaching" and the "dramatic monologue sermon.")

Robertson, Everett, comp. *Drama in Creative Worship.* Nashville: Convention Press, 1978. See "Dogma Is Drama," McEachern.

Robertson, Everett, ed. *Monologues for Church.* Nashville: Convention Press, 1982.

Sayers, Dorothy L. *The Man Born to Be King.* Grand Rapids: Wm. B. Eerdmans, 1943.

Speakman, Frederick B. *The Salty Tang.* Old Tappan: Fleming H. Revell, 1964. (See pp. 126-143 for two dramatic monologues.)

Steimle, Edmund A. Morris J. Niederthal, and Charles L. Rice. *Preaching the Story.* Philadelphia: Fortress Press, 1980.

TeSelle, Sallie McFague, "Parable, Metaphor and Narrative," *Homiletic,* vol. II, 1977, p. iii.

TeSelle, Sallie McFague. *Speaking in Parables.* Philadelphia: Fortress Press, 1975.